P9-CQF-007

Play That Preaches

Play That Preaches

52 Sermons for Children

Brant D. Baker

Abingdon Press

Nashville

PLAY THAT PREACHES
52 SERMONS FOR CHILDREN

Copyright © 2003 by Abingdon Press

All rights reserved.

No part of this work may be reproduced or transmitted in any form or by any means, electronic or mechanical, including photocopying and recording, or by any information storage or retrieval system, except as may be expressly permitted by the 1976 Copyright Act or in writing from the publisher. Requests for permission should be addressed to Abingdon Press, P.O. Box 801, 201 Eighth Avenue South, Nashville, TN 37202-0801.

This book is printed on recycled, acid-free, elemental-chlorine–free paper.

Library of Congress Cataloging-in-Publication Data

Baker, Brant D., 1958–
   Play that preaches: 52 sermons for children / Brant D. Baker.
      p.   cm.
   Includes bibliographical references and index.
   ISBN 0-687-06690-5 (pbk.: alk. paper)
   1. Children's sermons.   2. Sermons, American.   3. Children in public worship.   I. Title.
BV4315 .B254   2003
252'.53—dc21
                                                          2002015047

All scripture quotations unless noted otherwise are taken from the New Revised Standard Version of the Bible, copyright © 1989, Division of Christian Education of the National Council of the Churches of Christ in the United States of America. Used by permission. All rights reserved.

Scripture quotations marked CEV are from the Contemporary English Version, © 1991, 1992, 1995 by American Bible Society. Used by permission.

Scripture quotations marked RSV are taken from the Revised Standard Version of the Bible, copyright © 1946, 1952, 1971 by the Division of Christian Education of the National Council of the Churches of Christ in the United States of America. Used by permission. All rights reserved.

The children's sermons "Covenant" (originally "A Promise"), "The Armor of God" (originally "Temptation"), and "Independence Day" are reprinted by permission, *Children's Ministry Magazine*, Copyright 1995, 1996, Group Publishing Inc., Box 481, Loveland, CO 80539.

03 04 05 06 07 08 09 10 11 12—10 9 8 7 6 5 4 3 2 1

MANUFACTURED IN THE UNITED STATES OF AMERICA

To the children of
First Presbyterian Church
Mesa, Arizona,
especially Kellen and Gray

Contents

Introduction 11

Bible Stories

1. Covenant 23

2. The Holiest Place 25

3. Spying Out the Land 27

4. The Valley of Dry Bones 30

5. Acts of Praise 31

6. Going Up? (Praise the Lord!) 34

7. Blessed Are 37

8. Two or Three 39

9. The Greatest Commandment 41

10. Lost and Found in the Temple 43

11. Fruitful 44

12. Mercy! 46

13. A Friend at Midnight 49

14. A Prayer Fort (Good for a rainy day!) 52

15. Follow Me 53

16. Walking on Water 55

17. The Way 56

18. Vine, Branches, and Fruit 58

19. Free to Love 61

20. Smile! 63

21. One 64

22. The Armor of God 66

23. The Most Wonderful Thing 68

24. Running a Spiritual Race 69

25. Medic! 71

Church Year/Seasons

26. Wolves and Lambs 74
    SEASON/SUNDAY: ADVENT

27. The Shepherd's Story 76
    SEASON/SUNDAY: CHRISTMAS

28. His Name Is Wonderful 78
    SEASON/SUNDAY: CIRCUMCISION OF JESUS / NAME OF
    JESUS SUNDAY

29. Really Wise 81
    SEASON/SUNDAY: EPIPHANY

30. He Is Not Here! 83
    SEASON/SUNDAY: EASTER

31. Easter Eggs 85
    SEASON/SUNDAY: EASTER

32. Independence Day 87
    SEASON/SUNDAY: FOURTH OF JULY

33. What a Catch! 89
    SEASON/SUNDAY: EVANGELISM SUNDAY

34. Hip, Hip, Hooray! 91
    SEASON/SUNDAY: VOLUNTEER APPRECIATION

35. Love in Deed 93
    SEASON/SUNDAY: VOLUNTEER APPRECIATION

36. Serving Two Masters 95
    SEASON/SUNDAY: STEWARDSHIP

37. Ten Tenths 97
    SEASON/SUNDAY: STEWARDSHIP

38. Thank You! 100
    SEASON/SUNDAY: THANKSGIVING

39. King Jesus Is All 101
    SEASON/SUNDAY: CHRIST THE KING

Sacraments

40. Go, Make, Baptize, Teach 104
    BAPTISM (OR EVANGELISM SUNDAY)

41. Dizzy! 106
    BAPTISM

42. Rooted and Grounded 107
    BAPTISM

43. The Imitation of Christ 109
    LORD'S SUPPER

44. The Emmaus Road 112
    LORD'S SUPPER

45. One Loaf 114
    LORD'S SUPPER

46. Neither Greek nor Jew 116
    LORD'S SUPPER

Mother's and Father's Day

47. Mama, Do You Love Me? 118

48. A Good Wife, Who Can Find? 120

49. Honor Your Mother 122

50. Choose This Day Whom You Will Serve 124

51. A Father's Voice 126

52. Still Working 127

Bibliography 130

Index 131

Introduction

Christians at Play

From time to time, in the middle of doing a children's sermon, I've caught myself saying, "Now everyone gets to play!" This spontaneous way of inviting the entire congregation to participate must also belie how I really view what we're doing: we're playing. Now, the preacher part of me knows that there is "more" going on than simple play. But perhaps a deeper, more theologically insightful part of me knows that play, fundamentally and by God's design, involves a good bit "more" than we usually assume.

The "more" that's going on would seem to have something to do with the notion of recreation or re-creation. Recreation can be understood theologically as *being made again in the image of God*. As such, it is a handy parallel for what we understand about worship. The shorthand definition of worship is "to remember who we are and whose we are." Said another way, in worship we come to be re-created in the divine image. Could it be that when I invite the entire congregation to "play" what I really have in mind is an invitation to "re-creation," wherein we are "being created again in the image of God?" It seems likely.

So how does this happen? In his excellent book *Godly Play: A Way of Religious Education*, Jerome Berryman notes that Jesus gave us the best answer. "Become like a child,

[Jesus] said, if you want to mature as an adult. To play the ultimate game, don't rely on will, belief, denial, or reason alone. Play. Play in a Godly way. Play with the Creator. Enter the existential game with imagination, wonder, and laughter if you want to become new without end" (p. 17). Berryman then goes on to note that one of the places we play this existential game most intentionally and best is in the church. "There," he says, "the game is called 'worship' " (p. 17). Romano Guardini agrees, saying that worship "is a kind of holy play in which the soul, with utter abandonment, learns how to waste time for the sake of God" (Miller, p. 158).

Let's consider a few ways in which children's sermons enable this worshipful, becoming-like-a-child, godly play, to re-create us into God's image.

Letting Down Our Guard

There is benefit in distraction. A friend of mine told me about his former tennis coach who spoke of "the law of dominant effect." By it the coach meant that, as humans, we can really only think of one thing at a time. Therefore, while trying to remember all twenty-seven things the coach has told you to do, the reality is that you will remember one thing only, and it will likely be the last thing on the list of twenty-seven.

The application to community is clear. The law of dominant effect suggests that while we are concentrating on the "game," we will tend to let down our carefully constructed masks, we will tend to let wobble our precisely erected barriers, and by the time we're aware that our guard is down, new relationships will have emerged that no longer require these defenses. This distractional method of relating is behind everything from little league sports to fraternity initiations to corporate team-building outings.

Re-creation into the image of God is given a great boost when we dismantle our own creation of self. The "law of dominant effect" suggests that as we "play" we can only remember one thing, either to maintain our defensive constructs, or to enter into the game. The decision to enter into the game frees us momentarily from our constructed self, and when the game is over, we see ourselves and those around us in a new light, or perhaps more properly said, in a new image—the image of God. It is admittedly a slow process, but that sometimes seems to be the way God likes to work.

Overhearing the Gospel

The famed church father Augustine was powerfully moved after overhearing a child's game. One day while in a garden, mourning his inability to act more like the Christian he claimed to be, he heard the voice of a child playing next door. The child's game involved the chant, *"Tolle lege, tolle lege"* or "take up and read." Augustine went to a bench where there was a copy of the New Testament, and opened it to a verse that met his situation and need exactly. It was a profound turning point for the great scholar, one he would liken to Paul's Damascus road conversion. It came about because he "overheard" God's word to him (Bainton, p. 125).

One of the strongest arguments I know for keeping young children in worship is that they learn the prayers, hymns, and rhythms of liturgy while they are coloring on the bulletin. They aren't paying attention, but they "overhear" that which is presumably not aimed at them. This became clear one day as I preached the "adult" sermon. I asked a question, a common rhetorical device, to which no answer was expected. But seven-year-old Bradley didn't know the rules of rhetoric. He heard the question, looked up from his coloring, and rang out with the correct answer.

Communicators of children's sermons have long recognized the Augustinian aspect of adults "overhearing" the gospel, listening in on that which is not intended for them and thus being more free to hear it. It seems likely that this "overhearing" of that which we might otherwise screen out is that much more greatly enhanced if we are distracted by being part of the community at play. Just as Bradley heard and responded to the question while he colored, blissfully unaware of the conventions of rhetoric, so adults who are invited to "play" will "overhear" and respond.

It might be noted that adopting such a stance would get us further down the road in the tired debate of whether the children's sermon is for the children or really a sneaky way to "get at" the adults. The answer, of course, is that children's sermons do both; just as "adult" sermons are for the adults and also a sneaky way to "get at" the children.

Learning by Doing

Another reason to play together is that we learn best by doing. Inviting the adults to play during the children's sermon has the same benefit for them as for the children: *we remember best what we've not only processed with our eyes and ears, but also with our entire bodies.*

In this sense, is it going too far to suggest that there is a sacramentality to our play? Perhaps so, although it's an intriguing idea. At the very least there is an incarnationality to our play that resonates well with what God seems to be about: the Word becoming flesh is a core affirmation of what our life in Christ represents. Just as God put on flesh to teach us and save us, so too we are invited to put on flesh to learn and be saved.

This incarnationality of play is recognized by educators. The pedagogical hierarchy runs thus: tell me what to do and I'll remember 20 percent; show me what to do and I'll remember 30 percent; let me do it and I'll remember 90 percent. When we play together we learn in our flesh, and in so doing enter into an incarnational mystery that borders on sacrament. Good liturgy demands that praise of God and proclamation of the good news occur in a variety of ways— music, drama, silence, visual arts, as well as verbal communication—using the variety of gifts God has given us in the body.

A Sacrifice of Joy

Learning is, of course, only one part of our time in worship. Our comments until now have focused on the pedagogical aspect of sermons because that tends to be the overwhelming function of this kind of communication. In a larger view of worship, however, we come not only to learn, but to give our sacrifices of praise to God. In this enlarged understanding of worship, the children's sermon can provide us with some of the best time in worship: less structured, spontaneous moments when joy, laughter, and delight spill forth as our spiritual worship.

One of the more puzzling aspects of developing an appropriate theology of worship is trying to figure out what God likes. Is God a God of awesome mystery, holy decorum, and deep silence; or is God a God of down-to-earth approachability, holy hilarity, and joyful noise? The answer, of course, is *both*. That being the case, we often struggle in worship to balance all of these apparently paradoxical contradictions. It is possible, and at times even desirable, to explore the awesomeness of God during a children's sermon. But the children's sermon seems like a time well suited to exploring the joyous, playful side of God's nature. Faces light up, smiles appear, and as we play together we "enjoy God."

The Particular Nature of Community

Another paradox of our faith has to do with the struggle between that which is personal and that which is public. American culture seems especially intent on playing up the personal (which too often means "private") aspect of our faith, while losing sight of the public, or corporate, nature of our life together. We often tend to think of ourselves as individuals who come to church to carry out a personal religious duty. We rarely see that it is precisely in community that a unique religious reality is created that otherwise could not exist. Moreover, this unique religious reality of being "community" or "the Body of Christ" seems to be a thing that ranks especially high with God. Read the Bible and see: there is a lot more space devoted to the community than to the individual.

Of course we get a hint of this from the revealed nature of God. By coming to us as a Trinity, God seems to be making a statement about the importance of community. The fact is that we live out our relationship with God most strikingly in relationship with one another.

While it may give us a theological jolt to think of the Trinity as somehow "playful," the point still stands that "play" is much more readily achieved in community than solitarily. Thus when we play together in worship we manifest community in unique ways. And as we play as a community, we draw closer to the playful, triune God.

Nuts and Bolts—The Four Steps of Children's Homiletics

Experiential, hands-on teaching methods avoid the usual object lesson format for children's sermons. As I discuss in my previous two books, *Let the Children Come*, and *Welcoming the Children*, children from ages two to eleven do not yet possess the ability to think in abstract ways. But abstract thinking is exactly what is required to make the interpretive leap from an object to a biblical or moral truth. To show a five-year-old a pinecone and suggest that, just as it plants many seeds, so we too, as Christians, have many seeds to plant, is to miss out on two counts: how we are like pinecones, and what it means to plant seeds. Five-year-olds are concrete thinkers and need concrete truths.

Experiential teaching means just what it sounds like: we have an experience, and the experience is what teaches us. Many of the lessons so intended still require a kind of thinking that may be over the heads of the five-year-old, but the point is that they will be more likely to internalize the experience for later processing than they will an object lesson. As suggested above, the learning by doing route is the percentage winner in education.

What follows, then, are four steps to creating experiential sermons for children (in which adults are invited to play!) learned in over twenty years of presenting children's sermons.

Step One: Have a Text

Children's sermons do not preach well without a text. If it is hard to build an "adult" sermon around a scanty text, trying to pull together a children's sermon under similar circumstances is well nigh impossible.

But one week I was really stuck. I was working through a series on the twelve disciples, trying to draw from each one some aspect of discipleship. But there is precious little material to be had on some of the disciples, and this particular week was one of those. The story before us concerned the call of Nathaniel from under the fig tree. In the context of my series on discipleship I hoped to make this slim text a commentary on the importance of prayer.

Before you judge this as a fanciful departure from the text you should know that the commentators suggest a fig tree functioned in Middle Eastern culture as a kind of meditation room. The small houses lived in by most people did not afford much privacy, and so a fig tree, with its compact and lush growth pattern, was planted outside the front door—a shady, private retreat from the busy domestic engineering going on inside.

But where would I take all of this interesting (if somewhat tenuous) exegetical material when it came to the children's sermon? Despite years of doing "experiential Christianity" with children, I confess a tendency to set aside my "adult" sermon preparations when I come to prepare for the children's sermon. Typically I go back to the text and hope something more appropriate for the children will jump out.

But this week I was really stuck. With so little biography

on Nathaniel, trying to paint a picture of him as a disciple was out, even if one could think of a way to make that "experiential" for the children. His call from under the fig tree isn't particularly good drama, so enacting the story was out. I'd recently done something else that focused on prayer, so I was reluctant to head back in that direction.

As I floundered (and grew more panicked!) my "adult sermon" exegesis slowly seeped back in to consciousness. A fig tree, a private place—a fort! Maybe I was helped by the fact that it was a rainy weekend and I knew what my own children were up to back at the house, but, whatever the case, the idea bubbled up of bringing sheets from home and having the kids make a fort among the pews. From there we were off and the rest of the children's sermon unfolded (see "A Prayer Fort," p. 52).

Step number one in preparing children's sermons is to have a text. Children's sermons must take Scripture seriously enough to be based on it. Not only will it save us from trite moralisms and shallow object lessons, but, more to the point, it will lead us to the Spirit's life-giving truths and make true re-creation possible.

Step Two: Spend Time Brooding

The story of the struggle with the Nathaniel sermon illustrates what former Princeton Seminary preaching professor Don McCloud taught about the importance of brooding. The first step in sermon preparation, McCloud suggested, is to read the text. The second step, prior even to consulting commentaries and word studies, is to simply sit and make note of whatever stray ideas, comments, and questions that come to mind. Later, when it comes to actually writing the sermon, much of this material will not, and should not, make it in. But buried in an unlikely memory that floated to the surface while engaged in this brooding process will be the beginnings of a key illustration. Standing just off to the side of an exegetical question that came to mind is a central insight into what the text is really about.

It was McCloud's advice to spend at least an hour in this brooding process en route to writing a twenty minute "adult" sermon. So why shouldn't we budget a quarter of that time for a five minute children's sermon? Especially when we know that everyone—children and adults alike—will play? I would suggest that even fifteen minutes spent in "brooding" over the children's sermon unlocks more creative ideas than can be used in a month. Moreover, sometimes these insights find their way back into the "adult" sermon. Thus the entire exegetical process is enriched, and the entire preaching task (including both the children and "adult" sermons) works synergistically.

Brooding is a good place to find creative material because brooding is spiritual work: the word *inspired* is from the Latin, *in spirare* (breath, but with etymological connections to *Spirit*: thus to be *inspired* is to be *in the Spirit*). Beyond all this, being created in the image of God means that we share the ability to create. Jürgen Moltmann notes that the Old Testament term used to describe the creative activity of God is *bahrah*, a term used exclusively of God and never of the creative work of humanity. Thus the creative God plays with God's own possibilities "and creates out of nothing that which pleases him." Humans, on the other hand, "can only play with something which, in turn, is playing with [us]" (p. 18). Moltmann's sense is that even as we create, God invites us into a spiritual game in which we ourselves are both the players and the objects of God's playfulness.

Step Three: Dream Big

A corollary to brooding is dreaming big. Out of the brooding period will come some "normal" ideas and some pretty outrageous ideas. Start with the latter! I would submit that the best ideas are those that we are at first tempted to reject as too grandiose, or needing too much arrangement. In my experience, these ideas are usually manageable if I stick with them long enough to see how they can be carried out.

For example, I was looking for a way for the children to experience something of the shepherds' surprise and excitement on that first Christmas. But the story is so familiar, how could we really experience it anew? Asking the experiential question, I began with, "What would happen if we were to become shepherds?" So far so good, but one of the next questions became, "How can we have a huge angelic chorus?" Ready to dismiss this as a technological impossibility, it suddenly occurred to me that the congregation, with a small measure of advance notice (delivered in the bulletin) would do rather nicely as angels. From there, "The Shepherd's Story" was off and running (see p. 76).

And speaking of running, another example of dreaming big can be seen in "Running a Spiritual Race" (p. 69). Paul's text is clear, but how could we experience it with the children? Once committed to the idea of somehow running a race, the elements of this contest fell into place. Had I abandoned the idea, we would have missed the chance to play!

In this same regard, part of "dreaming big" is attending to children with special needs. The sermon "Running a Spiritual Race" meant accommodating a boy with a physical disability and a girl who is visually impaired. Other sermons, such as Father's and Mother's Day sermons, require sensitivity to children without the parent in question.

If possible, call the parents (or grandparents) of special needs children to alert them to what is planned for the coming Sunday, and to request their assistance. Having someone you can call on short notice to help in the middle of a sermon is also not a bad idea. In my experience, most adults in the congregation will jump into service if asked—after all, it allows them to play all the more!

Step Four: Look for Playful Moments

Specifically, look for playful moments where adults can also be invited to play. The best sermonic communications are those that include everyone. While I am not always successful in this element, sometimes it is simply as easy as inviting the adults to repeat the action, chant, or yell that the children have just been taught. Sometimes it can be more than that, with the adults providing important background elements for the sermon.

Consider "The Valley of Dry Bones" (p. 30). This is a simple re-enactment sermon (and one that is great fun for the children since it involves lying on the church floor!). But the adults enjoy it too as they are invited to make the sound of rattling bones (no comments on how adults would know this sound so well!), and then the sound of wind blowing once the bones are together. Everyone gets to play, and in ways that give each person a memorable experience of Ezekiel's great vision of God's re-creative work.

Jerome Berryman ends his book by noting that many adults learn, as adults, that their sense of identity has been covered over by what others have demanded of them. In contrast, there is an inner child awaiting discovery, who is "full of energy, creative, spontaneous, and deeply centered. . . . Godly play," suggests Berryman, "is a way to keep open the opportunity for the true self to emerge in childhood and the possibility that adults may return to where they began and begin to grow again" (p. 158).

Within the existential game of worship, children's sermons give us one opportunity to follow Jesus' advice and become like children. Here we are recreated. Here are opportunities for new relationships achieved as we are distracted in our fun. Here are possibilities for adults *and* children to overhear the gospel. Here are chances to learn by doing, the best way to learn. Here are occasions to bring a sacrifice of joy into the house of the Lord. Here are promises of experiencing the particular nature of community so central to our lives as Christians. All of this seems very, very good.

Let the children play!

Let *all* God's children play!

Bible Stories

1. Covenant[1]

Scripture: *Genesis 17:1-8*

Focus: *God's covenant, or promise, is the basis of our human promises. We are free to create relationships of trust because of what God has already done for us.*

Experience: *Everyone will see the risk, vulnerability, trust, and commitment that are part of any strong relationship.*

Arrangements: *You will need a sturdy length of rope, and an adult who will help demonstrate a promise of trust before the children try it.*

Leader: Good morning! How many of you have ever made a promise?

Children: Me! I did! I promised to take care of my friend's kitten.

L: And did you keep the promises you made?

C: (responses)

L: Do some people keep promises better than others?

C: (responses)

L: Good. Well, I'm going to ask John to come up here and help me. John, you take one

---

1. Reprinted by permission, *Children's Ministry Magazine,* Copyright 1995, Group Publishing, Inc., Box 481, Loveland, CO 80539.

	end of this rope, and I'll take the other. Now I'm going to promise I won't let go, and I want you to do the same. Do you promise not to let go?
John:	Yes.
L:	Okay, I'm going to lean back and hold on to the rope, and I want you to do the same (both of you hold on to the rope and lean back so that each is supported by the weight of the other). What would happen if John or I broke our promise?
C:	You'd fall!
L:	That's right, and not just one of us, but both of us, because we're both leaning back! Does anybody else want to try it?
C:	Me! I do!
L:	[Obtain volunteers and necessary promises! It is advised that the leader or the adult keep hold of one end of the rope (that is, avoid putting children on both ends of the rope). Continue conversation as children experiment.] So, what would happen if either John or Katie let go?
C:	They'd fall!
L:	And they'd probably get hurt, too! Promises are like that: If one person doesn't keep their promise, both people get hurt. Well, if you were going to have to stay holding on to this rope forever, I guess you'd want someone who was big and strong and who would be able to keep that promise to hold on forever. I wonder who is like that?
C:	God? My daddy?
L:	Your daddy?! That's nice! God? Yes I think so. What are some of the promises that God makes to us?

24

C: To love us, to save us, to forgive us, to always be with us.

L: Those are great answers—okay, let's stop holding the rope and hold hands and thank God for being so trustworthy in our lives, and for teaching us how to be trustworthy, too. *(Prayer)*

2. The Holiest Place

Scripture: *Exodus 26:34 (also ties in to Psalm 134)*

Focus: *This sermon focuses on the notion that anywhere we find God is a holy place. This sermon gives children permission to prowl around in, and subsequently demystify, areas that may normally be "off limits" to them (chancel, pulpit, choir loft), and then seeks to enlarge the concept of "holy space" to everywhere in the sanctuary and beyond—wherever God is found.*

Experience: *The children will look for the holiest place in the sanctuary.*

Arrangements: *None are needed, but you may want to think through the logistics of the "search" for the holiest place. Will you keep the group of children together, or split them up and send them off (if you choose this latter option you may want to have assistants ready to help lead these "search parties")?*

Leader: Good morning! It's great to see everybody. Say, I have a question for you. I was reading in Exodus about the building of the tabernacle, which was really a kind of movable church, and in the instructions God tells the people of Israel to put the Ark of the

	Covenant in "the most holy place." That got me to thinking, what is the holiest place in our church?
Children:	The pulpit. The place where they baptize. The table. The place where my daddy sits.
L:	Hmmm. All of those sound like they might be good answers. I suppose the only way to really be sure is to get up (motion to children to get up) and go and look! Let's look first at the baptismal font, since it's right here. Seems pretty holy, and I know we've had some special moments here. Better keep it high on our list. Okay, let's go check out the Communion table. What do you think, is this a pretty holy place?
C:	Yes!
L:	Okay, well, we'll keep that on our list, too. Okay, someone said the pulpit. Let's go look at that. Wow, you don't usually get to see what's back here. Hmmm. If it's a holy place it's a holy place that needs a good cleaning. We have a few paper clips, this broken pencil, a bulletin from—three months ago, and this empty flower vase. I don't know, do you think this is a holy place, even though it's so messy?
C:	Yes. No.
L:	Well, I suppose that even messy places might be holy places if God is there. Okay, one of you said that where your dad sits is holy, but I suppose any place out in the sanctuary where a holy Christian is sitting might be a holy place. Let's go check out some of the pews (do this as long as you have time). While you do that, Kellen, would you come with me and we'll go check out the choir

	loft. Hmmm, what do you think, is this a holy place?
Child:	(nods)
L:	(Re-gathering children) So, what do you think, did we find the most holy place?
C:	Yes. No. They're all holy.
L:	Say, there's an idea! They're all holy. How come?
C:	Because God is there.
L:	Wow, that's a great insight! I think you're right. Any place God is, that's going to be a holy place—whether that's the Communion table, or a messy pulpit, or even the place where you're going to go back and sit. Let's have a prayer and thank God for making holy places out of so many of our places by being there. *(Prayer)*

3. Spying Out the Land

Scripture: *Numbers 13*

Focus: *Everyone will become a part of the drama of the Israelites' initial exploration of the promised land, and in so doing, understand some of the challenges, risks, and rewards in trusting God.*

Experience: *We will enact the spies' entry and their report to the children of Israel.*

Arrangements: *None are needed, but give some thought beforehand to how you will divide the adults in the congregation, and the sanctuary itself, between the inhabitants of the promised land (a larger number and area) and the Israelites (a smaller number and area).*

Leader: Would the children please meet me in the middle of the sanctuary? This morning we're going to talk about a time in the Bible when the children of Israel first came out of the desert and looked over what they called the promised land (begin walking children around sanctuary as if "in the desert" while recounting the story of the exodus). They had escaped from Pharaoh, and had made their way to the land God had *promised* to give them. Boy, were they excited. When they finally came to the promised land they stopped (stop at the boundary of the area you have determined to be the "promised land" part of the sanctuary). They chose spies to go in and scout out the land. Hmmm. I think all of us should go in (send in *all* the children amongst the pews, encouraging them to explore).

That's good exploring and spying. Okay spies, let's get back together here in the aisle (reassemble children). Great! Well the story we have in the Bible says that the spies brought back with them a bunch of fruit, including a single cluster of grapes that was so big it had to be carried on a pole between two of the spies! (Load children down with imaginary fruit and begin walking back to the "children of Israel" section of the sanctuary.)

When the spies got back to the main camp they said to the people (lead the following dialogue antiphonally), "It's a good land."

Children (as spies): "It's a good land."

L: (leading the "Children of Israel" section of the adults, excitedly) "Ohh!"

Children of Israel Adults: "Ohh!"

L: (ask the promised land adults to stand up and look menacing): "But the people are big."

C (spies): "But the people are big."

L: (turning to Children of Israel adults, dejectedly) "Ohh."

Children of Israel Adults: "Ohh."

L: Now, God had promised, *promised* the people this land, that's why it was called the "promised land." Do you think God would have given it to them?

C: Yes.

L: But most of the people didn't trust God's promise, and as a result, they didn't get what God had promised. There were two spies, though, who said, "Let's go!" Do you think you would be like one of those spies who trusted God and said, "Let's go"?

C: Yes! Let's go!

L: Good! Well sometimes it's hard to trust God's promise, but God is always faithful, and those two spies did get to go into the promised land. Well, let's have a prayer, and how about, at the end of our prayer, I'll say "God, when you say you will keep your promise, help us to say . . ." and then you all say, "Let's go!" *(Prayer, concluding as indicated above)*

C: Let's go!

4. The Valley of Dry Bones

Scripture: *Ezekiel 37:1-10*

Focus: *This sermon shows how the power of God can bring to life that which is dead and dry.*

Experience: *This sermon is full of great fun for everyone. The children lie on the floor (something that seems to delight them), and then slowly come to life, while the congregation makes all sorts of fun sounds!*

Arrangements: *None.*

Leader:	Good morning! Wasn't that an interesting Bible story we just heard? Well, we're going to act it out right now, so first I need someone to be the prophet Ezekiel. Okay, Joshua. Now the rest of us get to lie down and pretend that we're just a bunch of dry old bones. Great! Now in the story, God comes to Ezekiel and asks if the bones can live, and Ezekiel gives a really good answer. He says, "GOD, you know."
Child (Ezekiel):	"GOD, you know."
L:	Then God tells Ezekiel to prophesy to the bones and say this (if you know "Ezekiel" can read comfortably, ask him or her to do so out of the Bible you will supply, otherwise, have the child repeat back the words that you speak quietly into his or her ear).
Child:	"O dry bones, hear the word of the LORD. . . . I will cause breath to enter you, and you shall live. . . . And you shall know that I am the LORD."

L: Good, now we need the congregation to start making some quiet wind sounds. Good, and then a growing wind sound. Good, and then a kind of rattling. Good, now you bones here on the floor, you need to start to stir a little, just move a little bit around as life comes into you. Good, now a little more wind, and a little more moving. Good, then Ezekiel said,

Child: "Thus says the Lord GOD; Come from the four winds, O [Spirit], and breathe upon these—that they may live."

L: And so there was even more wind, and more rattling and more movement, and then the Bible says that breath came into them and the bones lived, and they stood on their feet (motion children and congregation to rise), and there was an exceedingly great host (motion to congregation for wind and rattling to stop if it doesn't do so on its own). (Enjoy a brief moment of silence to drink in this experience.) Let's have a prayer and give thanks for the life giving breath of God's own Spirit in our dry bones as well. *(Prayer)*

5. Acts of Praise

Scripture: *Psalm 100:4*

Focus: *This sermon teaches the actual actions behind several Hebrew words associated with worship. We come to find out that worship is a much more physical exercise than many people imagine!*

Experience: *The children and congregation will learn four actions of worship.*

Arrangements: *None.*

Leader: Good morning! Let me read you a verse from the Psalms that talks about how we are to praise God: "Enter his gates with thanksgiving, and his courts with praise. Give thanks to him, bless his name." Wow! Did you hear all those actions?

Children: No!

L: You didn't? Well, that's probably because the action words are in Hebrew, the original language of this psalm. Let me explain them to you. We probably better stand up so we can do all the things it says we're supposed to do.

Okay, the first one is "enter God's gates with thanksgiving." The Hebrew word there is *todah*. The word means to give thanks with upraised hands. It's a word for **thanksgiving,** but it's also an action. So let's all raise our hands and say *todah*.

C: (raising hands) *Todah!*

L: Perfect! The next one is **praise** and the word there is *tehilaw*. That word really means a hymn, but it also comes from a root word that means to celebrate, or even to rave and be foolish. Hmmm. Maybe we should keep our hands up in the air, and wave them around while we sing a celebration song, maybe just the first part of "Joyful, joyful, we adore thee."

C: Joyful, joyful, we adore thee (waving hands in the air).

L: You know, that was pretty good, but don't you think it would be even better if the congregation played with us? Everybody up! Okay, from the beginning, *todah*.

All: *Todah!*

L: Joyful, joyful!

All: (while waving hands) Joyful, joyful, we adore thee!

L: Okay, this is getting good now! The next word in Psalm 100:4 is *yadah*. It gets translated as **give thanks**, and that's fine, but it's another word that has an action too, and the action is to extend our hands, like we're saying thanks (extend hands).

All: *Yadah!* (extend hands)

L: And then the last word is the word *barach*, which is **to bless**. And here again, we have a word that is also an action, and the action is to kneel as an act of adoration. Probably there's not enough room in the pews for everyone to kneel, but (to the children) we can, can't we?

C: Yes! (kneeling)

L: Okay, one more time, from the beginning, and that will be our closing prayer. I'll read the verse, and we'll all do what we now know the words are telling us to do. Ready? "Enter God's gates with **thanksgiving**."

All: *Todah!* (hands raised)

L: "And God's courts with **praise**."

All: Joyful, joyful, we adore thee (waving hands).

L: "**Give thanks**."

All: *Yadah!* (extending hands)

L: "And **bless** God's name."

C: *Barach!* (kneel)

L: Amen!

6. Going Up? (Praise the Lord!)

Scripture: *Isaiah 2:3, Luke 2:22, Matthew 20:17-18*

Focus: *This sermon focuses on the word "up" as a verbal reminder to praise the Lord. As such it is in line with monastic practices that seek to integrate faith and life through reminders, auditory and visual, scattered throughout the day. Think of it as a spoken WWJD bracelet!*

Experience: *The children will learn about the Jewish practice of* alihay *(the pilgrimage of "going up" to Jerusalem) and hear the response "Praise the Lord" every time the word "up" is mentioned.*

Arrangements: *None are needed, but you'll have to be on your toes for this one (don't worry, the children will catch you if you're not!). The goal here is to say "Praise the Lord" or some other phrase of your choosing every time you say (or hear) the word "up."*

Leader:	Good morning! Will the children please meet me in the middle of church? Good to see you! I have a question for you: what do we say if we are going that way (point to front of church)? Would we say something like, "Let's go *down* there?"
Children:	No!
L:	So, what would we say?
C:	Let's go *up* there.
L:	(under breath, "Praise the Lord") Good! And let me ask you something else: Do you ever hear your mother or father say, "I'm going up ("Praise the Lord") to the corner store to get some milk?"
C:	Uh huh. We don't have a store on the corner. Why do you keep saying that?

L: And do you ever say something like, "I'm going to go up ("Praise the Lord") to the park and play with my friends"?

C: Yes, no, why do you keep saying that?

L: Saying what? (If children don't prompt, ask them if they notice, then continue.)

C: Praise the Lord.

L: Oh, that. Well I was thinking this week about the city of Jerusalem. The Bible talks about people "going up" ("Praise the Lord") to the city of Jerusalem, and it is up ("Praise the Lord") on a kind of mountain or high plain. In fact, Jewish people try to make an *Aliyah* at least once during their lives. *Aliyah* is the Hebrew word that speaks of "going up" ("Praise the Lord"), and at least once in their lives devout Jews will try to make their way "up" ("Praise the Lord") to Jerusalem. Well, we may never make an *aliyah*, but what if we used the word "up" ("Praise the Lord") to remind us to "Praise the Lord," every time we heard it, especially since we seem to use the word "up" ("Praise the Lord") a lot? Do you want to give it a try?

C: Yes!

L: Okay, we'll start easy. I'll read some verses from the Bible that talk about going up. . . .

C: Praise the Lord!

L: Good! And as I read you say what you're supposed to say; and congregation, you can play too! This first verse is from the prophet Isaiah. "Many peoples shall come and say, 'Come, let us go up . . .

C: Praise the Lord!

L: . . . . to the mountain of the LORD, to the
       house of the God of Jacob; that he may
       teach us his ways and that we may walk in
       his paths' " (Isaiah 2:3). That was great!
       Okay, here's one about Jesus and his par-
       ents. "When the time came for their purifi-
       cation according to the law of Moses, they
       brought him up . . .

C: Praise the Lord!

L: . . . to Jerusalem to present him to the
       Lord" (Luke 2:22). Very good! Okay, one
       last one, about Jesus and his disciples.
       "While Jesus was going up . . .

C: Praise the Lord!

L: . . . to Jerusalem, he took the twelve disci-
       ples aside by themselves, and said to them
       on the way, 'See, we are going up [try not
       pausing to prompt this time and see if the
       children catch this second "up"] to
       Jerusalem, and the Son of Man will be
       handed over to the chief priests and scribes,
       and they will condemn him to death' "
       (Matthew 20:17-18). Very, very good! Okay,
       so here's your assignment. This week, when-
       ever you catch yourself or someone else say-
       ing "up" . . .

C: Praise the Lord!

L: Try to remember about going up . . . to
       meet the Lord, and say "Praise the Lord!"
       Let's have a prayer and thank God for this
       way to remember our faith. *(Prayer, ending
       somehow with the word "up")*

C: Praise the Lord!

7. Blessed Are . . .

Scripture: *Matthew 5:3-10*

Focus: *This sermon leads us to understand the truths of the beatitudes experientially. A case can be made, following some exegetes, that each beatitude builds toward the next.*

Experience: *Everyone will go through a series of simple motions that relate to each beatitude.*

Arrangements: *None.*

Leader:	You are all looking rather blessed this morning! That's what the word beatitude means, it's a kind of blessing, or blessedness. I want to teach you eight of the blessings that Jesus taught in the Sermon on the Mount by showing you a motion for each one. Ready?
Children:	Ready!
L:	Okay, the first one is "Blessed are the poor in spirit." When I hear that I think of someone who might be on their knees, looking down, realizing that they are poor inside, in their spirit. Let's all get on our knees, look down, maybe even fold our hands.
C:	(move into position) I'm not poor, I have a quarter!
L:	A quarter! That's great! And, many of us aren't poor inside either, but Jesus seems to say that this is where a lot of people start. Congregation, you don't have to kneel, but why don't you join us in the rest of these motions? Okay, The next beatitude is "Blessed are those who mourn." Does anybody know what it means to "mourn"?
C:	Like getting up in the morning?

L: Well, actually it means to be sad, and I
    think that Jesus means we're blessed if we're
    sad about our sin. What do you do if you're
    really, really sad?

C: Cry.

L: That's right, so let's all stay on our knees,
    and make a crying motion, like we're crying
    over sin. That's great. Next Jesus says,
    "Blessed are the meek." To be meek means
    to be humble, and it may mean that after
    we are sad over our sin, we humbly accept
    God's forgiveness, so maybe we could look
    up with a "thank you" on our faces.

C: Thank you!

L: Absolutely, we can even say that can't we!
    Okay, the next thing Jesus says is that peo-
    ple who hunger and thirst for righteousness
    are blessed. Hmmm. What do you do when
    you are hungry?

C: Eat!

L: That's right. And how do we eat righteous-
    ness?

C: (make eating motions)

L: I think we might pretend to eat God's word.
    We'd never really do that, but let's pretend
    we're eating a "Bible sandwich" because
    we're so hungry for God's righteousness.
    Wow, I'm full! Okay, what do you think we
    could do for the next beatitude, "Blessed are
    the merciful"? What's mercy?

C: Being nice. Forgiving. Loving.

L: All good answers, and I'm thinking if we
    just put our arm around another person, it
    would be a way for us to show that we are
    forgiving, loving, and comforting them.
    Great! "Blessed are the pure in heart" is

next. How about we stand like we are praying, looking up, thinking pure, clean thoughts? That's great, next is "Blessed are the peacemakers." (Pick two children and position them facing each other while explaining.) Peacemaking is something we are sometimes called to do when we see others having a disagreement or getting ready to fight. Let's say these two children were getting ready to argue (direct children to have angry faces). What could we do? (Take a third child and place him/her between the other two.) We could come between them and look at them with the love of God. Of course, sometimes even peacemakers can get hurt, and I think that's why the last beatitude Jesus offers is, "Blessed are those who are persecuted." And that's what happened to Jesus when he brought peace to us: he was put on the cross (have everyone point to the cross in the sanctuary).

(If you have time you might want to run through all of these postures again quickly. Otherwise close in prayer.) *(Prayer)*

8. Two or Three

Scripture: *Matthew 18:20*

Focus: *Our cultural setting tends to privatize worship. People come for an individual experience that they wrongly believe has little to do with anyone else who might be present. But the Bible makes clear that worship is a radically social phenomenon. While there is a place for worship in our private devotion, corporate worship creates and attains spiritual realities that are simply not possible when we are alone.*

Jesus didn't say, "Wherever one is I am there among them." Jesus said, "Where two or three are gathered in my name, I am there among them."

Experience: *The children will experience "worship" in a variety of configurations and decide which works best, both experientially and in keeping with Jesus' words.*

Arrangements: *None.*

Leader:	Good morning! I am *so* glad I'm not here alone this morning! Are you glad you're not here alone?
Children:	Yes. No.
L:	Not everyone is sure, and even if you are sure, let's try an experiment. Everybody stand up, and congregation, you can play too, everybody stand up! Good, now spread out a little bit, and feel like you're standing alone, good. Now, I'd like you to worship God by singing a hymn or song—it doesn't matter what you sing, but don't sing what anyone else around you is singing. Everybody start singing! (Leader, be sure to participate, if only to break the silence!) Okay, you can stop now. Did that feel very worshipful?
C:	No!
L:	No, and did it fulfill what Jesus said in Matthew 18:20? Oh, you probably need me to read it to you: Jesus said, "Where two or three are gathered in my name, I am there among them." Can Jesus be *in the midst* of one standing all alone?
C:	No!
L:	Okay, well, let's try something else. Everyone get into pairs (allow a moment for

pairs to form, and watch for solo children so that no one gets left out). And now start singing again, only this time agree between the two of you what you will sing. (Again, leader should be paired and singing.)

Okay, did that feel more worshipful than when you did it alone?

C: Yes!

L: And can Jesus be *in the midst* of two?

C: Yes!

L: I think so too. But let's try one more thing. How about if your pair joins another pair, or even two other pairs, and agree together what you will sing (give a moment for this arrangement). Great! Now sing! (Leader paticipates.)

So, did that feel even more worshipful? And can Jesus be *in the midst* of many?

C: Yes! Yes!

L: I think so too! And now you know why I said I was glad I wasn't here by myself this morning! Let's have a prayer and thank God that something special happens when we come together that can't happen when we're just by ourselves. *(Prayer)*

9. The Greatest Commandment

Scripture: *Matthew 22:36-40*

Focus: *This sermon focuses on the complexity of trying to remember all the commandments, versus the simplicity of Jesus' summary of those commandments.*

Experience: *The children will be asked to remember the Ten Commandments, and then learn Jesus' summary of all the commandments.*

Arrangements: *You will need a large piece of poster board, cut in the shape of two connecting tablets (the typical representation of the tablets upon which the Ten Commandments were received), or a chalkboard or markerboard. If you use this latter set up, draw two large tablets on the writing surface. Whatever writing surface you use, an easel will make the presentation of this sermon easier!*

Leader: Great to see everyone. I've got a tough question for you. Can you remember all of the ten commandments? I've got a couple of tablets here, and I'll write them down as you call them out.

Children: Don't lie. Don't cheat. Don't steal. Honor your mother and father. Don't kick. Don't kill. Love your neighbor as yourself. Don't argue. Don't covet. Don't be mean. Don't swear.

L: Hmmm, well, that's eleven! It's hard to remember them all, isn't it, and sometimes it even seems like there are more than ten! But did you know that Jesus gave us a simple way to remember all these commandments? (Turn poster board tablets over, or erase the board list.) He said there were really only two: "love God" (write on one tablet), and "love your neighbor as yourself" (write on other tablet). (Expand as desired or simply end with prayer.) *(Prayer)*

10. Lost and Found in the Temple

Scripture: *Luke 2:41-52*

Focus: *The story about the boy Jesus being "lost" after his bar mitzvah ends in a curious twist: he is actually not lost at all, but is "found" in the temple. The focus of this sermon is on how we can be "found" in God's house, no matter how lost we might be.*

Experience: *Everyone will help look for someone who is "lost."*

Arrangements: *Contact a child or adult late in the week (preferably someone the children know well) and ask for his or her help. Arrange with them to go and hide somewhere in the sanctuary while the children are coming forward for the children's sermon. You don't have to know where they choose to hide, but it might not hurt! If so desired, ask the "hider" to be ready to respond with the line, "Did you not know that I must be in my Father's house?" (Luke 2:49b).*

Leader:	Good morning, it's great to see everyone! Say, I need your help this morning, it seems that Gray is lost! Let me look around and be sure. Nope, I don't see him here—do you?
Children:	No!
L:	So, just as I feared, he's lost! I think I saw him earlier though, so I'm pretty sure he's in here somewhere. Let's go look for him! Everybody get up, and spread out. Some of you go over that way, some of you look over there, and Susie, will you and Cynthia go look in the choir—they look suspicious, like they could be hiding something. Let's

	see, why don't you come with me and let's look up here. Look really close; look in the pews, around people's feet. (Gray is hiding on the floor under a pew.) Any luck?
C:	No!
L:	Well, keep looking, he's got to be in here somewhere.
C:	Here he is!
L:	You found him? Great, let's all go over there. Gray, we've been looking all over for you. *We thought you were lost* (cue line).
Gray:	"Did you not know that I must be in my Father's house?"
L:	Well, you know, now that you mention it, that does make sense: you weren't lost, you were right where you were supposed to be all the time. Wow. Let's have a prayer and thank God that we can never be lost if we're where God wants us to be. *(Prayer)*

11. Fruitful

Scripture: *Luke 8:4-15*

Focus: *This sermon focuses on the amazing fruitfulness God has designed into creation. That fruitfulness includes our own call to sow seeds of invitation to hear the gospel, and is well illustrated in that the "smallest seed" can bear big fruit!*

Experience: *The children will pretend they are seeds, and will watch their fruitfulness spread throughout the congregation.*

Arrangements: *None.*

Leader:	Good morning! It's great to see you, especially because you're all looking so fruitful!

The story we just heard is about a sower—
someone who plants seeds—and about what
happens with those seeds. Do you remember
some of the bad things that happened to
some of the seeds?

Children: They got eaten by the birds. The weeds got
them. They couldn't grow on the rocks.

L: That's right—you were really listening! But
what happened to the last group of seeds?

C: They grew!

L: They grew and gave back hundredfold!
That's a lot! It's like cutting open a pumpkin
and finding hundreds and hundreds of
seeds. And if only part of those seeds were
planted well and grew, there would be hundreds and hundreds more pumpkins, and
thousands and thousands more seeds, and
past that my brain can't do all the math!

Well, this morning we're going to pretend
that we're seeds! Everybody stand up and
start to feel seedlike. I'll pretend I'm the
sower, and I'm going to fling you out into
the congregation (make flinging motion as if
sowing seeds). I'd like each of you to go
stand at the end of a pew. Go ahead (flinging with hand), find one where no one else
is standing. Does everybody have a pew?
Good!

Okay, now, I'd like you to hold up four
fingers. Those four fingers will represent the
four things that can happen with seeds. Now
the first three fingers represent bad things
that can affect seeds: rocks, weeds, and birds.
But one of those fingers is fruitful, and I want
you to offer that fruitful seed to the first person in the pew, and say to them, "Jesus loves

you." And if you're being offered that fruitful finger, would you please take it and hold on to it? Good—everyone gets to play today. Now, would the first person in each pew hold up four fingers on their other hand, turn to the person next to you, say, "Jesus loves you," and let the next person grab your one fruitful finger, and so on down the pew until everyone is linked together.

So how about that little seeds! You went out and gave growth to a hundredfold harvest! Let's have a prayer and thank God that we can all be fruitful for Jesus Christ. *(Prayer)*

12. Mercy!

Scripture: *Luke 10:30-37*

Focus: *This sermon looks at the familiar parable of the good Samaritan, and uses the story to suggest three ways of showing care:* sympathy—*"I'm sorry you hurt" (priest);* empathy—*"I'm sorry you hurt and I hurt with you" (Levite);* compassion—*"I'm sorry you hurt, I hurt with you, and I'll work to do something about it" (Samaritan).*

Experience: *The children will enact the parable of the good Samaritan.*

Arrangements: *None.*

Leader: It's wonderful to see everyone today, and we need to get right to it! We're going to pretend we're in ancient Israel, on a very dangerous road that runs down a deep valley between Jerusalem and Jericho. There are steep cliffs and lots of caves where even today some pretty mean people hide out to rob people who might be walking on that road. Jesus told a story about a man who was walking down that road and got robbed and beaten. Let's see, who would be willing to be that man—we promise we won't hurt you!

Child: I will!

L: Okay, Kelley, lie down right here. Now, in the story Jesus says that three people came by, one at a time, and saw the man. Who will be the first?

C: Me!

L: Okay, Katelyn, the first one to come by was a priest. Jesus said the priest saw the man, so walk along and see our victim. Then the Bible says the priest walked by on the other side of the road; so move away. Good. Katelyn, do you suppose the priest was sorry that the man got hurt?

C: Yes/no.

L: (If "no") Well, would you be sorry?

C: Yes.

L: Yes, I think he was sorry the man got hurt, but that was all, he wasn't going to get involved. Now Jesus says the next person to walk by was a Levite. Any Levites here?

C: I am!

L: I always thought so! Okay, Bryan, good, you're the Levite, and you walk along, and you see the man who was beaten and robbed, and Jesus says that he also moved over to the other side of the road (help guide child if necessary). And do you suppose he cared?

C: Yes.

L: I think so, and he might have even cared more than the first peson, enough that he wasn't only sorry that the man was hurt, but he found himself hurting a little too. Can you look like you hurt? Maybe pretend to cry a little? Good! Okay, now a third man came by in the story Jesus told, who will be that man?

C: Me!

L: Great, Ashley, and Jesus said that this man had *compassion* for the hurt man. What does it mean to have compassion?

C: To care, to love.

L: Yes, all those things, and also to care enough and love enough to get involved and try to help the man. Jesus says that the Samaritan tended to the hurt man's wounds (guide child to enact story), loaded the man on his donkey (you could draft an adult "donkey" here, or just pretend) and took him to an inn, like a hotel. (Quickly locate another child to be the innkeeper.) John, will you be the innkeeper? Great. The Samaritan paid the innkeeper to take care of the hurt man, and promised to take care of any other expenses he might have. Now, which of the three do you think did the best job of loving his neighbor—the one who was sorry, the one who was sorry and hurt, or the one who was sorry and did something?

C: The last one.

L: That's right, and that's the kind of care and love and compassion Jesus wants us to show to other people, too. Let's have a prayer and thank God for the abilities we have to show that kind of care. *(Prayer)*

13. A Friend at Midnight

Scripture: *Luke 11:5-8*

Focus: *This sermon focuses on God's honor in answering prayer. The sermon turns on a crucial insight by Kenneth Bailey concerning the true meaning of the parable of the friend at midnight (*Poet and Peasant, *pp. 119-33). While this parable is frequently interpreted as a call for persistence in prayer, Bailey wonders what kind of God would be grumpy with us when we interrupt his sleep, and has to be persistently pestered before finally "getting up" and granting our needs. In contrast Bailey suggests that this is a parable about honor. In the ancient Middle East (as today), hospitality was a high virtue. For a friend to be so dishonorable as to not meet such a simple request (for bread) was unthinkable. Jesus is telling a "compare and contrast" kind of parable: "If your friend knows enough about honor to meet your need, how much more honorable is God." This meaning becomes clear in verse 13: "If you then, who are evil, know how to give good gifts to your children, how much more will the heavenly Father give the Holy Spirit to those who ask him!"*

Experience: *The children will hear the story of the friend at midnight told in all its unbelievability, and then experience the surprise of how different God is from such a friend.*

Arrangements: *You will need to think through the "geography" of the sanctuary to determine the best place for the children to go hear the story of the friend at midnight. Such a place, ideally, would feature a door that could be knocked on, and through which a friend could eventually appear. A second, similar, location is also needed. A volunteer, arranged* *beforehand, will need to move into that second location behind the closed door, unobserved by the children. The volunteer, posing as God, has only one line (see below).*

Leader: Good morning. Let's go over here to this little door. Let's pretend this is the door to someone's house. Any volunteers to be inside the house? Okay, John, this is now John's house, and let's have two or three others go in as your children (you may not want to close the door all the way if there is some danger here of escape or mischief!).

Great! Now, we need a friend of John's. Okay, Keesha. Here's a story Jesus told: One night, very late, Keesha had some unexpected guests. She didn't have anything to feed them, so in a panic she rushed over to John's house and knocked on the door (indicate for child to knock). From inside John said, "Who's there and what do you want?"

Child: "Who's there and what do you want?"

L: Keesha replies, "John, I've got unexpected company and nothing to feed them. Could I borrow a loaf of bread?"

C: "John, I've got unexpected company and nothing to feed them. Could I borrow a loaf of bread?"

L: According to Jesus, in this story John says something unbelievable. John says, "Don't bother me! My door is locked, the children are all tucked in, and so just go away."

C: "Don't bother me! My door is locked, the children are all tucked in, and so just go away."

L: Now, says Jesus, can you imagine any friend being as rude and thoughtless as that?

C: No!

L: No, most of our real friends would never do such a thing. (Start moving to the second location as you continue talking. Be sure to get "John" and his family before you leave!) No, our real friends would know that if they don't get up, everyone would be talking the next morning about how rude they were.

(Arriving at second door where volunteer is hidden inside) Jesus told this story to compare such a friend with the way God works. Do we have to knock and knock and knock on God's door, hoping God will get up and not be too grumpy with us?

C: No!

L: No, we know that God isn't like that friend. How is it that we knock on God's door?

C: By knocking . . . ?

L: Well, yes, and we knock on God's door by praying—by folding our hands and saying "Dear God." Let's do that together, at the count of three, and see what happens: fold our hands, and one, two, three . . .

C: Dear God.

Volunteer: (on cue) "Yes?"

C: (surprised!)

L: Wow! And that's just how God is—good and trustworthy, and always ready to hear our prayers. So let's have a prayer and give thanks for that. *(Prayer)*

14. A Prayer Fort (Good for a rainy day!)

Scripture: *John 1:43-51 (also Matthew 6:6)*

Focus: *Apparently within the human heart there is a drive to go to places that are safe and cozy. The focus of this sermon is to suggest that such places are also places where God is present.*

Experience: *In this sermon you'll build a sheet fort in the sanctuary and then discuss prayer.*

Arrangements: *Bring two or three large sheets, depending on the size of the group and the proposed location of your fort.*

Leader:	Good morning, or should I say, "rainy morning"? What kinds of things do you like to do on rainy days?
Children:	Sleep, eat, read, make forts!
L:	Make forts! That's what I used to like to do on rainy days. In fact, when I saw it was raining today I decided to bring some sheets from home for us to make one (or, "Just thinking about it made me decide to").
C:	Oh boy!
L:	Let's ask the people here in the first two rows to stand up and move, and then let's drape the sheets from the back of this pew to the back of that one (supervise fort building; some nearby adults may need to hold sheets on the slippery pews). Wow! What a great fort. I guess the only thing that's left for us all to do is get in (join children inside as best you can!). This is so nice and cozy, and it feels so safe. What do you do in your fort once

you've gone to all the trouble to make it?

C: Sleep, eat, read, play dolls, tell stories.

L: Those are all great and fun things to do. But did you know there is one other thing you can do in a fort like this, where we feel safe and cozy? We can pray! (Reference scripture. If about Nathaniel, mention how the tree Jesus saw him under was a common feature in Jesus' day, and a place where people often went to get away and find quiet for prayer. If Matthew text, talk about the importance of a quiet, private place where we can talk honestly to God.)

Well, since we're here, let's have a prayer too, and give thanks for cozy, quiet places where we can go to talk with God. *(Prayer)*

15. Follow Me

Scripture: *John 1:43*

Focus: *This sermon focuses on what it means to follow Jesus (who leads us in unexpected ways), to minister to others, and eventually to arrive at the cross or table.*

Experience: *Children will be asked to follow the leader around the worship space, even when there are unexpected twists and turns!*

Arrangements: *None are needed, but you might want to give some thought to the "route" you will take to have the right amount of time for talking through this sermon with the children.*

Leader: Good morning, will all the children please follow me? (Begin walking up an aisle or wherever your route leads.) I've got a question for you: What did Jesus mean when he said to his disciples, "Follow me"?

Children: That they should go where he went, that they should follow him.

L: I think you're right (take the children out into the narthex and circle around, or make a sudden U-turn). Jesus asked the disciples to follow him on an exciting journey, going places they had never been before, doing things they had never done before. Oh, let's go over there (cut across chancel or choir loft). Pardon us (to worshipers). Well, let me ask you another question, what kind of things did Jesus' disciples do on their journey?

C: Prayed, ate, slept, learned, helped people.

L: Exactly right! They did all those things. (At this point in your "journey" plan to head down a row of seats.) And even if sometimes they might have stepped on people's toes, their basic mission was to learn from Jesus how to love people and spread God's good news. Say, why don't we love these people right here? (Lead children in saying things like "God loves you" and "God bless you" and in giving hugs.)

(Lead the journey now toward the Communion table or the cross.) And where did Jesus finally lead his disciples (arriving at Communion table or cross)?

C: To the last supper. To the cross.

L: Right, to the place where Jesus gave himself for them, and for all people. Let's have a prayer and give thanks to God that we are all called to follow Jesus, too. *(Prayer)*

16. Walking on Water

Scripture: *John 6:16-21*

Focus: *The storms of life often make us afraid (or sick—see the comment below made by a child!). The focus of this sermon is the way Jesus calms our rocking boat when we let him get in with us.*

Experience: *The children and adults will recreate the scene where Jesus walked to the disciples on water during a storm.*

Arrangements: *None are required, but if you wanted to enhance the experience, tape together several pieces of cardboard to create the outline of a boat (large enough to fit all your children inside). Use pieces of cardboard a foot or so wide, or as long as you can find. Join them end to end and fold around to form the "sides" of a boat. (Use the same boat made for the sermon "What a Catch," or save the boat from this sermon to use in that one!)*

Leader: Will all the children please meet me in the middle of the sanctuary aisle? Good morning, great to see you! This morning we're going to act out the story we just heard: it's about one day when Jesus went off to pray and the disciples got in a boat to go across the lake. Would someone be willing to be Jesus? Okay, thanks Lauren. Why don't you go up here to pray (position child in chancel area or elsewhere). Now the rest of us are going to pretend that we're the disciples in the boat, and we're crossing the lake. Everybody sit down here in the aisle, and maybe pretend like you're rowing the boat. Hmmm, well, okay, we don't all have to row the same way I guess—sounds like the disciples! Now, this is a really big lake that the disciples were going across, and sometimes they have really big storms, so you can feel the boat starting to sway (help the children get into this movement). And the wind was starting to blow (instruct the congregation to make blowing and other storm sounds), and the waves were getting bigger, and the boat was swaying more, and the wind was blowing harder, and the waves were getting bigger (children are rocking more and more), and the wind was blowing harder"

Children: I think I'm getting seasick!

L: . . . and the disciples are getting seasick, and they're also becoming afraid. And then, they look, and *as if* they weren't already afraid enough, they see Jesus walking toward them (motion for "Jesus" to get up and start walking toward the boat). But as soon as Jesus got into the boat, the wind stopped (motion to congregation to stop their blowing sounds), and it says that immediately the boat was at the place they were going!

Wow! Let's have a prayer and thank God that when we let Jesus into our lives, the storms stop and we get to where we need to go. *(Prayer)*

17. The Way

Scripture: *John 14:6-7*

Focus: *What does he mean when Jesus says he is the way, the truth, and the life? This sermon focuses on an answer to that question, suggesting that the* *"way" of Jesus is to show us to the Father, not simply to tell us how to get to the Father.* This message is basically an enactment of an illustration given by William Barclay in his commentary on this passage (The Gospel of John, *vol. 2, p. 157).*

Experience: *The children will be given complex directions to an unnamed objective, then asked if they would prefer the leader to be the "way" for them, to lead them to the place they are being asked to go.*

Arrangements: *None are needed, but think through the directions you will give. The goal here is to make the directions complex, and to obscure the final destination, which should be a significant symbol in the sanctuary (for example, the Communion table, a cross, or a stained glass window depicting the crucifixion).*

Leader:	Good morning! Great to see everyone. Well, did anyone bring a paper and pencil to write down some directions, or maybe someone has a compass?
Children:	No!
L:	Well, that's okay, just listen close, here's what I'd like for you to do. Go down the aisle here to the fifth pew and then turn left. Go across the row and turn right when you get to the end, and then come to the top of that aisle and go right. When you've gone as far as you can, go right again. When that comes to an end go left, then a sharp right, and then right again. Then you'll be there, okay? Great, get going!
C:	Huh? Where? Can you say that again?
L:	Hmmm, I guess that was a little hard to

follow. Say, would you like me to lead you instead?

C: Yes!

L: (Set off on the course described.) Well, I don't mind doing that at all, and that's really what I wanted to talk with you about. What do you suppose Jesus meant when he told his disciple that he is the "way"?

C: He is how they should go?

L: Yeah, that's right. (Continue walking as you talk, timing your remarks to your arrival at the symbol you have chosen for a destination.) And to show them how they should go, Jesus came and lived with us. You see, Jesus didn't just stay up in heaven, calling down instructions to us like "Go left there and right here." Instead, he came down and lived among us. He didn't just teach us about being good, he showed us by being good himself; he didn't just tell us to love people, he loved people himself; he didn't just tell us to follow and obey God's will, he followed and obeyed God's will himself (arriving now at the table/cross/window) even to the point of giving his life, so that we might have our life in him.

Let's have a prayer and give thanks to our Lord Jesus Christ for being the way, the truth, and the life for us. *(Prayer)*

18. Vine, Branches, and Fruit

Scripture: *John 15:1-11*

Focus: *This sermon is focused on the rich imagery that compares our relationship with Jesus to the relationship of the vine, branches, and fruit. As is often* *the case, Jesus uses the somewhat abstract power of narrative to bring forth a point that is, in many ways, deeper than words.*

Experience: *In this sermon the children will experience the church family as the "branches" they pass through to become "fruitful."*

Arrangements: *There are a number of ways to set up this sermon, depending on the size of your group and the nature of worship at your church (for example, formal or informal) and the time constraints of the children's sermon. You will need a sufficient number of adults to form one or two (or more if necessary) "branches" through which the children will pass on their way to bursting forth as fruit. These "branches," then, take the form of a kind of column or chute, with adults on either side. Some of the adults should adopt postures of prayer, some should speak words of encouragement, others can show compassion through touch, still others can say a scripture verse or two—all demonstrating the kinds of things churches do to encourage and bring to "fruition" the children and youth in their charge. While it might be possible to set this up on the spot, it is probably preferable to arrange it ahead of time (for example, with an adult Sunday school class).*

Leader:	Good morning! And may I say that you're all looking rather "fruity" this morning! That's a good thing! Let me ask my adult helpers to come forward and get in place, and let me ask the children to meet me in the main aisle here. Great. In the story we just heard, does anybody remember what Jesus said he is?
Children:	A branch? A vine? Fruit?
L:	Well, we've got all the main parts! Jesus said that he is the vine, the true vine, and that

we are branches bearing fruit. So I've asked
these adults to become two branches, and
can you see that they both are attached here
at this end to the aisle. Who do you suppose
the aisle represents?

C: Jesus.

L: That's right! Just like a tree trunk, Jesus is the
main support and supply for all of the
branches. Good. Now, Jesus says that the
branches are supposed to bear fruit, and
that's where you come in. You are some of
this church's fruit, and it's the responsibility
of everyone here to make sure you get to
burst forth like the good fruit you are. So, in
a grapevine or in a fruit tree, the fruit starts
out as juice in the main branch or trunk,
kind of circulating around (lead children to
become this kind of juicy sap), and when the
time is right, the juice makes its way toward
the branch (lead a child toward start of
chute). While the juice is in the branch of the
church it gets prayed over and loved and
taught (direct adults to carry out examples of
these actions) and given everything it needs
until it can burst through the end as fruit.

C: (Perhaps child walks through end of chute
rather dully.)

L: No, excuse me, that didn't quite get the job
done. Come back here to the end of the
branch, okay, now I said that the fruit
bursts through the end of the branch. Let's
see some bursting!

C: (Perhaps this time child leaps and throws
arms out wide.)

L: Great! Okay, now let's get all the rest of
that juice through the branches. Let's see

some bursting—great! But wait a minute, everyone stop! What would happen if the branch decided not to carry the juice from the vine?

C: No fruit could come out.

L: That's right. Or what would happen if the branch decided to disconnect from the vine (move end of the "branch" away from the aisle)?

C: No fruit. It would die.

L: Exactly so! (Reconnect branch.) So the branch needs to stay open and stay connected (direct action to continue), so the fruit can keep on popping out the end of all the branches in joyous celebration.

Let's have a prayer and thank God for giving us Jesus as the true vine, and one another as branches to bear fruit—and for the fruit, too! *(Prayer)*

19. Free to Love

Scripture: *1 Corinthians 8*

Focus: *We live in a culture obsessed with personal rights and freedom. This sermon focuses on the truth that, as Christians, our "right" is the right to love, and our "freedom" is the freedom to refrain from actions and words that cause others harm.*

Experience: *To "freely" do something that turns out to cause someone else a "problem."*

Arrangements: *Enlist an adult accomplice, presumably seated in one of the affected seats (see below), to say the line indicated below.*

Leader: Good morning! Hey, I've got great news! I got permission for us to take the hymnbooks out of these first few rows of pews and make a castle here on the chancel! Come on—let's start getting the hymnals out (begin this activity with help from the children), and some of you can start building (arrange this activity). Won't it be neat to use these hymnals to build a castle?

Children: Yes!

L: (continue patter about how tall, how big, design, and so forth, until the "cue line" for your adult helper, which might be something like . . .) "I wonder how tall we could make this castle if we got every hymnbook in here?"

Adult: (To leader) Uh, I'm glad you all could build your castle, and it's very nice, but how are we all supposed to sing the hymn later?

L: Well, um, you know, Pam, that's a good question. (To children) How will the people sing if we have all these hymnbooks up here?

C: They could come and get them. We could take them back.

L: We will take them back in just a minute, but you know, it makes me realize that, even though we were free to take them, what we did had an unexpected effect on someone else. I guess part of what it means for us to love other people as we would want them to love us is to think about our actions and make sure that there aren't any unexpected results from what we do. You think so? Well, let's have a prayer and thank God that we are able to use our hearts *and* our minds when we love others, and then let's get all these hymnbooks put back. *(Prayer)*

20. Smile!

Scripture: *1 Corinthians 12*

Focus: *While we affirm that all Christians have gifts, it can be difficult for children to know exactly what their gifts might be. Few children show signs of the gifts listed in the Pauline letters. The focus of this sermon is on one gift that children have that they might not even be aware of: a smile. The effect of using this gift with the congregation is quite powerful!*

Experience: *The children will explore gifts together, then use the gift of smiling to illicit smiles from the congregation.*

Arrangements: *None.*

Leader:	Good morning! Great to see all your smiling faces! Say, I want to ask you a question, do you have any gifts?
Children:	No. Yes. I got a doll for my birthday.
L:	Well, let me explain what I mean: The apostle Paul tells us that every person in the church has something special to offer to everyone else in the church, something that Paul calls a "gift." He says that some people can preach, and some people have wisdom, and some people can heal. In other places he says that some can be teachers, and some can be evangelists. So, my question is, do you have any of these gifts?
C:	No. Yes.
L:	I don't blame you for being unsure. To tell you the truth, those all sound like grown-up kinds of gifts. But did you know that you have a special gift, one that is especially for

children? (At this point turn off microphone if used, and whisper conspiratorially to children.) Your gift is the gift of smiling! Do you know how much power you have with your smiles? I want you to see, so in just a minute we're all going to stand up, and without saying anything, we're just going to smile out at the congregation, as big a smile as you can. You watch and I promise you that when they see you smile, they'll start smiling too! Okay, ready? One, two, three—let's all stand and smile!

C: (all rise and smile)

Congregation: (returns smiles as predicted)

L: (Turn microphone back on; return to normal voice.) Wow! Did you see that? We all smiled at them, and that was such a powerful gift that they all smiled back! That's a great gift that you have, and you can use it almost anytime and anywhere. Sometime this week, when you're out at a store with your mom or dad, and you see someone who looks like they need your gift, look right at them and give them a big smile! Let's have a prayer and thank God for this great gift that we have to give. *(Prayer)*

21. One

Scripture: *Ephesians 4:1-6*

Focus: *This sermon focuses on the oneness of the Body of Christ, and could be used with a number of biblical texts that speak to this theme. The goal of this sermon is to "wrap our arms around" this message!*

Experience: *The children will be invited to form progressively larger hugs, as we demonstrate the oneness of the Body.*

Arrangements: *None are needed; however, you may want to think about whether you will stop the demonstration with the children, or attempt to invite the entire congregation.*

Leader:	Good morning! Let's meet in the middle of the sanctuary so we can be ready to do something I've got planned. Okay, I've got a question for you—what are some of the ways two people show that they are one?
Children:	They say "I love you." They help one another.
L:	Those are good answers. Is there a way that they could actually show this, is there some action they could take (start cueing a hugging motion)?
C:	Hug!
L:	There you go! They could hug. So, could I have a couple of volunteers to hug? Great—Ashley and Megan. Okay, what if three people wanted to show that they were one?
C:	A bigger hug?
L:	I think so, who will join Ashley and Megan? Great, Suzanne, thank you. What if there were six people who wanted to show that they were one?
C:	An even bigger hug!
L:	You bet! So who will join? Okay, the three of you. But what if all of us wanted to show that we were one?
C:	Hug!
L:	Great, so let's do that, and while we're all

getting into a giant hug, let me ask this,
"What if we wanted to say that the whole
church was one?!"

C: A super big hug!

L: That's right, so everybody stand up.
Congregation, move in around this giant hug
(another option at this point might be to
hold hands), and let's have a prayer thanking
God for our oneness in Jesus Christ. *(Prayer)*

22. The Armor of God[1]

Scripture: *Ephesians 6:10-17*

Focus: *The Bible tells us that we should be alert to
the attacks of the Enemy. In whatever way your theology defines that Enemy, the Bible tells us that we
don't have to be victims, that God has provided for
our protection, that we can be "strong in the Lord."*

Experience: *Everyone will learn words and actions
associated with each piece of God's armor.*

Arrangements: *None.*

Leader: Good morning! I have a question for you:
What is temptation?

Children: When we do something wrong. Being bad.
A bad idea.

L: I like that last answer, "A bad idea!" Well,
temptation isn't actually what we do so
much as it is the idea to do something bad.
Temptation is about the bad ideas that
Satan puts in our head to try and get us to
turn away from God. But you know what?

---

1. Reprinted by permission, *Children's Ministry Magazine,* Copyright 1995,
Group Publishing, Inc., Box 481, Loveland, CO 80539.

The Bible says that we can defend ourselves by putting on the "armor of God." Everybody stand up, and let's learn what that armor is. I'll do a motion and say some words, and then you do what I do, okay? Here we go: the first part of the armor of God is the belt of truth. For that we'll put our hands on our hips, and say "No lies."

C: (putting hands on hips) No lies!

L: Good! You know, it occurs to me that everyone can play this: congregation, on your feet! Here we go, (hands on hips) "No lies."

All: No lies!

L: Good! The next piece of the armor of God is the breastplate of righteousness. So for this we'll beat our chest (demonstrate) and say, "Good deeds."

All: (beating chest) "Good deeds."

L: Good, from the beginning (indicate for all to join in unison). (Hands on hips), "No lies," (beat chest) "Good deeds." Great! Okay, next are the shoes. We'll stamp our feet and say, "Stamp Satan."

All: (stamping) Stamp Satan.

L: Okay, from the beginning: (lead with motions) No lies, good deeds, stamp Satan. Great! Now comes the shield of faith. So let's make a cross with our arms and say, "Have faith."

All: (motion) Have faith.

L: And from the beginning (review all motions). Super! Okay, next comes the helmet of salvation. For this let's put our hand on our head and say, "Been baptized."

All: (motion) Been baptized!

L: Once more from the top (review all). Okay,

last one. The only offensive weapon in the whole armor of God is the sword of the Spirit. For this let's open our hands as if they were a Bible and say, "God's word."

All: (motion) God's word.

L: Okay, one last time from the beginning (repeat). Wow, that was great! Let's have a prayer and thank God for the armor that protects us from temptation. *(Prayer)*

23. The Most Wonderful Thing

Scripture: *Philippians 3:7 as translated in the* Contemporary English Version *says, "nothing is as wonderful as knowing Jesus Christ my Lord."*

Focus: *The sermon is focused on the most wonderful thing we might know about Jesus.*

Experience: *The children will share the wonderful things we know about Jesus.*

Arrangements: *None.*

Leader: Good morning! Let me ask you a question: What's the most wonderful thing you know?

Children: My mommy loves me. I'm going to the circus. Jesus loves me.

L: Those are all wonderful things, but I wonder if we would all think that Jesus' love is really the *most* wonderful thing we could know?

C: (nod in agreement)

L: Okay, well, what do you know about Jesus?

C: That he loves us, that he died for us, that he forgives us, that he will take us to heaven.

L: Those were all good answers. I think maybe

we should give everyone a chance to play. Congregation, we invite you to turn to the person next to you and share the most wonderful thing you know about Jesus. (Continue similar conversation with children until time to pray.) Let's have a prayer and thank God for our wonderful savior Jesus Christ. *(Prayer)*

24. Running a Spiritual Race

Scripture: *Philippians 3:12-16*

Focus: *To use Paul's image of a "race" as a means to understand spiritual growth, and the disciplines that children might realistically pursue as part of this race.*

Experience: *To move around the sanctuary through three, four, or five stations, each supervised by one or more adult helper, and each featuring one brief activity that is a child-appropriate way to run the discipleship race.*

Arrangements: *You will need to decide what your stations will be, and then arrange for the necessary adult help for each one. In the example below the four stations were praise, prayer, proclamation, and* provision. *Consider finding adult leaders for the stations who have an interest in that particular area of the church's life. Thus, "praise" could be overseen by some choir members who could sing a short praise song with each group of children ("Praise Ye the Lord," "Jesus Loves Me," or something else simple); "prayer" might be led by someone who is part of the church's prayer chain who could have each group of children kneel and recite the Lord's Prayer; "proclamation" might be a leader in the* *congregation for outreach and evangelism who could have the children share the good news with surrounding adults by saying "Jesus loves you"; and "provision" could be overseen by the ushers, there with offering plates, where the children could be asked to "provide" by giving their offering for the day, or by suggesting children give an offering of hugs to those nearby.*

Note: If you have children with physical handicaps, be sure to find ways for them to be included, perhaps by contacting their parents ahead of time and asking them to accompany their child. You may also want to be alert to this as you ask your opening question and modify the sermon accordingly.

Leader:	Great to see everyone today. How many of you have ever been in a race?
Children:	Me! I have! I won third place once.
L:	That's super! Sounds like we have some experienced racers here. Well, here's another question: how many of you have run in a spiritual race?
C:	Huh?
L:	I didn't think so! So today we're going to have that chance. In just a minute we'll divide into four groups. Then I want you to go to your assigned areas and follow the instructions of the adults there, and proceed, clockwise (motion the correct way) around the sanctuary, to the next station. Will my adult helpers please get in place? (Count children off by number of stations and send them to stations.)
	(Let children go through circuit once, and have the congregation cheer each time a

group finishes. The cheering will be a cue to the adult leaders to know when to release their group—they shouldn't let their group go until they hear a cheer from each of the stations. When everyone has finished all four stations, lead a conversation about the experience.)

C: We won! *We* won! No way, *we* won!

L: Okay, okay. Let me ask you this, where do you see a finish line? There isn't one! Why isn't there a finish line?

C: Because you forgot to put one up? Because you never finish the race.

L: That's right, John, because you never finish running this kind of race. We just go back through the stations again, and then, once we've got these actions all figured out, we can move on to new challenges so that we can become really mature in our Christian faith. Let's have a prayer and give thanks that God keeps challenging us our whole life through. *(Prayer)*

25. Medic!

Scripture: *James 5:13-16*

Focus: *This sermon is focused on the church's role as a "hospital" for sin sick souls.*

Experience: *The children will play out two different scenarios—one involving physical injury (pretend!) and our response, the other involving spiritual injury (pretend) and our response.*

Arrangements: *None.*

Leader:	Good morning, good to see everyone. You're all looking well. Does everybody feel pretty good?
Children:	Yes!
L:	Hmm, well we still need a volunteer, someone who can pretend they aren't feeling too good. Any volunteers to be our pretend patient? Okay, Joanna, thanks. Good, now we need some other volunteers to be her friends. Okay, you three. Great, now everyone else gather over here as the hospital. Super! Okay (to patient), let's pretend that you were driving along and you get into an accident (briefly act out driving, wreck, lying on the floor injured). Oh boy, that looks bad. Now, some of your friends come along (get friends), and what do you friends do?
C:	Take her to the hospital?
L:	Exactly! (It's probably best to not try to carry the "injured" victim, rather, help her or him up and give support while limping to hospital.) So we take Joanna to the hospital, and there the doctors and nurses take care of her (lead the hospital staff through some basic motions), and then Joanna comes out well.
	Okay, let's pretend again (everyone return to original place), only this time let's pretend that Joanna is going along and has an accident with sin. Maybe she sees somebody and gets angry and hits him (act out, pretending with someone in a seat nearby) and so she sins; or maybe someone else sees Joanna and calls her a name. Either way, she's down again and hurting, because she's

been wounded with sin. Now her friends come along (get friends)—well, what do we do, where do we take her?

C: To the hospital? To the church?

L: Exactly, we take her to the church hospital! First Presbyterian Hospital, right here on Mesa Drive (substitute your own church's name and location). (As "friends" take "patient" toward the "hospital") You people that were the hospital, now you are the church. And what do the people there do for her?

C: Love her, pray for her, take care of her.

L: That's right. According to the book of James, if she needs to confess her sin, we listen to her confession, and then we can anoint her with oil, lay hands on her, and pray for her. Well, let's go ahead and lay one hand on Joanna, and one hand on someone else; and congregation, would you do the same, lay a hand on someone nearby, and let's thank God we have a place to bring the sin sick soul. *(Prayer)*

Church Year/Seasons

26. Wolves and Lambs

Scripture: *Isaiah 11:1-10*

Season/Sunday: *Advent*

Focus: *This sermon creates a picture of the church as a partial fulfillment of the prophet's vision—that in the day of the Lord, those who are normally enemies of one another "will not hurt or destroy on all my holy mountain."*

Experience: *The children pretend to be different animals that are "natural" enemies in order to experience the vision of the kingdom of God as presented by the prophet Isaiah.*

Arrangements: *None.*

Leader: Good morning! We're getting closer and closer to Christmas, and as we do, we are hearing again the Old Testament prophecies about how the coming of Jesus Christ would change things forever. One of those prophecies is about how different animals, who usually don't like one another, will someday get along.

So, let's pretend that we're some of those animals. Everyone stand up. Who would like to be a wolf? Who wants to be a leopard, a lion, a bear, a snake? (Send wolves, and all animals in this first group, into an area close by on your left.) Okay, and who would like to be a lamb, a baby goat, a calf, a cow, and a baby? (Send those in this second group to an area close by on your right.) Okay! Now, everyone make the sound your animal makes!

Children: (make sounds)

L: Now let me ask you, do these animals over here (point to animals on left) get along with these over here (point to group on your right)?

C: No!

L: You're right, they don't, at least in the world out there (indicate world outside the church walls). But in here (point to the children), in here they do. So, why don't we have the wolf (or wolves) come and hug the lamb(s), and the leopard(s) hug the baby goat(s), and the calf hug the lion(s), and the cow(s) hug the bear(s), and even the baby hug the snake!

We know this kind of thing doesn't happen out there (indicate out in the world), but it does happen in here (indicate church) with people who are like these animals. The coming of Jesus Christ changes relationships. Look out there (point to the congregation). Do you see any wolves or leopards or bears (no pointing!)? Do you see any lambs or kids or cows? Of course you do! Men and women, rich and poor, black and

white, strong and weak—we have a whole
church full of different animals that get
along together, because of the coming of the
baby Jesus. Let's have a prayer and thank
God that we worship in this special kind of
place. *(Prayer)*

27. The Shepherd's Story

Scripture: *Luke 2:8-20*

Season/Sunday: *Christmas*

Focus: *This sermon focuses on the shepherds as the
first witnesses and worshipers at our Lord's birth.*

Experience: *The children will "be the shepherds" the
night of Jesus' birth.*

Arrangements: *First, you need an angel to read Luke
2:10b-12. Then arrange for the organist to play the
"Gloria" from "Angels We Have Heard on High."
Finally, consider having a crèche set up somewhere in
the sanctuary.*

Leader:	Will the children please join me here (some-where away from the crèche). This morning we're going to pretend that we're the shepherds who were watching their flocks the night Jesus was born. And you know, some of them may not have been much older than some of you. What do you suppose they were doing as they were out in the field that night?
Children:	Talking, eating, sleeping.
L:	Could be. My guess is that they were also trying to keep warm, so maybe we could pretend that there's a fire here, and we're kind of cold. They were probably just mind-

ing their own business (cue line for angel narration) when all of a sudden an angel appeared.

Angel: "Do not be afraid."

L: But I think they were afraid (act afraid, cower, bow on a knee, and so forth).

A: "Do not be afraid; for see—I am bringing you good news of great joy for all the people: to you is born this day in the city of David a Savior, who is the Messiah, the Lord. This will be a sign for you: you will find a child wrapped in bands of cloth and lying in a manger." (The organist should begin playing a verse of "Angels We Have Heard on High" underneath this narration. As the reading ends, and organ swells to chorus, signal the congregation to stand and become the heavenly host by singing the "Gloria" chorus).

Congregation: (singing) "Glo-o-o-o-ria, in excelsis Deo. Glo-o-o-o-ria, in excelsis Deo!"

L: (Motion congregation to be seated.) Wow! Do you think the shepherds were impressed? An angel telling them the good news, an angelic chorus singing glory to God in the heavens? Wow! So, what did the shepherds do next?

C: They went to find the baby!

L: That's right! So let's go. (Make way to crèche; while traveling continue with . . .) Isn't it amazing that the first visitors to visit the King of heaven were lowly shepherds like us?

C: Uh-huh.

L: (arriving) What do you suppose they did when they got to where Jesus was?

C: Worshiped him, prayed, sang "Happy
      Birthday."

L: What great ideas! Let's sing "Happy
      Birthday" to Jesus, and then have a prayer
      thanking God for sending us this great gift.
      (Prayer)

28. His Name Is Wonderful

Scripture: *Luke 2:21 (and many others)*

Season/Sunday: *Circumcision of Jesus / Name of
Jesus Sunday (usually the last Sunday in the year)*

Focus: *This sermon is about the many names for
Jesus. It borrows from popular posters and songs
that are devoted to this wide variety of names and is
designed to expose the children to these many biblical ways of relating to our Lord.*

Experience: *The children will hear names for Jesus
read by members of the congregation.*

Arrangements: *You will need to provide a copy of
the list provided on page 80 to readers throughout
the congregation (permission is granted to photocopy
"The Names of Jesus" page). Provide each reader
with the full list, with one name highlighted for them
to read. You may also want a second copy of the list,
cut up into strips, to provide the children with one of
the names of Jesus, and the verse where that name is
found, to take back to their seat with them.*

Leader: Good morning! It's absolutely terrific to see
           everyone this morning! Well today we lis-
           tened to a story about the day that Jesus
           was named. In his day and culture, a little

boy was taken to the temple when he was
eight days old, and the priest would bless
him and give him the name his parents had
chosen. But did you know that the Bible
also gives us lots and lots of other names for
Jesus? Can you think of some of them?

Children: Christ. Savior. Jesus.

L: Right! Those are some of the other names of
Jesus. But there are *lots* more! Here are
some of them (cue for first reader to stand).

Readers: (read from list of names)

L: Wow! Did you ever think there were that
many different names for Jesus? And every
one of those names gives us another way to
think about who Jesus is for us and how we
can be in relationship with him! Let's have a
prayer and thank God for this wonderful
gift of names, and then I have something to
give you. *(Prayer)* (Distribute slips with
names of Jesus, inviting children to think
about that particular name throughout the
week, perhaps using it when they pray.)

The Names of Jesus

Instructions to Readers:

You are asked to read aloud the name highlighted below during the children's sermon. The leader will call for the list and the names will be read in order. When your turn comes, please stand and say the name loudly! There is no need to read the verse that accompanies the name.

ROCK The LORD is my **rock**, my fortress, and my deliverer, my God, my rock in whom I take refuge, my shield, and the horn of my salvation, my stronghold. (Psalm 18:2)

FORTRESS The LORD is my rock, my **fortress**, and my deliverer, my God, my rock in whom I take refuge, my shield, and the horn of my salvation, my stronghold. (Psalm 18:2)

DELIVERER The LORD is my rock, my fortress, and my **deliverer**, my God, my rock in whom I take refuge, my shield, and the horn of my salvation, my stronghold. (Psalm 18:2)

SHIELD The LORD is my rock, my fortress, and my deliverer, my God, my rock in whom I take refuge, my **shield**, and the horn of my salvation, my stronghold. (Psalm 18:2)

THE HORN OF MY SALVATION The LORD is my rock, my fortress, and my deliverer, my God, my rock in whom I take refuge, my shield, and **the horn of my salvation**, my stronghold. (Psalm 18:2)

WONDERFUL COUNSELOR For a child has been born for us, a son given to us; authority rests upon his shoulders; and he is named **Wonderful Counselor**, Mighty God, Everlasting Father, Prince of Peace. (Isaiah 9:6)

MIGHTY GOD For a child has been born for us, a son given to us; authority rests upon his shoulders; and he is named Wonderful Counselor, **Mighty God**, Everlasting Father, Prince of Peace. (Isaiah 9:6)

EVERLASTING FATHER For a child has been born for us, a son given to us; authority rests upon his shoulders; and he is named Wonderful Counselor, Mighty God, **Everlasting Father**, Prince of Peace. (Isaiah 9:6)

PRINCE OF PEACE For a child has been born for us, a son given to us; authority rests upon his shoulders; and he is named Wonderful Counselor, Mighty God, Everlasting Father, **Prince of Peace**. (Isaiah 9:6)

BREAD OF LIFE Jesus said to them, "I am the **bread of life**. Whoever comes to me will never be hungry, and whoever believes in me will never be thirsty." (John 6:35)

LIGHT OF THE WORLD Again Jesus spoke to them, saying, "I am the **light of the world**. Whoever follows me will never walk in darkness but will have the light of life." (John 8:12)

GOOD SHEPHERD "I am the **good shepherd**. The good shepherd lays down his life for the sheep." (John 10:11)

PASSOVER LAMB Clean out the old yeast so that you may be a new batch, as you really are unleavened. For our **[passover] lamb**, Christ, has been sacrificed. (1 Corinthians 5:7)

CORNERSTONE So then you are no longer strangers and aliens, but you are citizens with the saints and also members of the household of God, built upon the foundation of the apostles and prophets, with Christ Jesus himself as the **cornerstone**. (Ephesians 2:19-20)

THE ALPHA AND THE OMEGA "I am the **Alpha and the Omega**," says the Lord God, who is and who was and who is to come, the Almighty. (Revelation 1:8)

LION OF THE TRIBE OF JUDAH Then one of the elders said to me, "Do not weep. See, the **Lion of the tribe of Judah**, the Root of David, has conquered, so that he can open the scroll and its seven seals." (Revelation 5:5)

ROOT OF DAVID Then one of the elders said to me, "Do not weep. See, the Lion of the tribe of Judah, the **Root of David**, has conquered, so that he can open the scroll and its seven seals." (Revelation 5:5)

KING OF KINGS AND LORD OF LORDS On his robe and on his thigh he has a name inscribed, **"King of kings and Lord of lords."** (Revelation 19:16)

From *Play That Preaches* by Brant D. Baker. Copyright © 2003 by Abingdon Press. Reproduced by permission.

29. Really Wise

Scripture: *Matthew 2:1-12*

Season: *Epiphany*

Focus: *Sometimes we lose the impact of strong biblical language due to translation. Nowhere might this be more true than with words having to do with worship (see "Acts of Praise," p. 31). The story of the Magi's visit includes the Greek word* proskuneo, *which is used to denote awe, wonder, and reverence, and includes the ideas of falling prostrate on the ground and even kissing the ground before a deity.*

Experience: *To lie down and "kiss" the ground before Jesus.*

Arrangements: *None are necessary, but you may want to move the crèche to an accessible place, perhaps the chancel.*

Leader:	Good morning, let's all gather around the crèche. Great to see everyone today! Do you know why we call this a crèche?
Children:	(silence, maybe a few guesses)
L:	Well, the word crèche is French, and it means crib; and of course, that's what this is—a crib. Jesus was probably long out of his crib by the time this story takes place. Lots of people think that by the time the wise men got to Jesus, he was about two years old. The wise men had a long way to go! And what did they do when they finally got to where Jesus was?
C:	Gave him presents!
L:	That's right, they gave him presents. The presents were part of their way of worshiping

Jesus. But there was also something else that
they did. Listen again to what the Bible story
says, "And going into the house they saw the
child with Mary his mother, and they fell
down and worshiped him" (Matthew 2:11
RSV). Did you hear it? What did they do?

C: Fell down, worshiped him.

L: That's right! They fell down and worshiped
Jesus. The word there is a Greek word,
proskuneo, and one of the things that it
means is to fall down flat and worship. Do
you suppose we should try that? I mean, we
probably can't do that every time we come
to church, because there are all these pews
and things, but since Jesus is here, let's
spread out so everyone has room. Good,
and let's get down flat with our face in our
hands. Now, there's something else about
this word *proskuneo,* it doesn't just mean
falling down flat, but it can also even mean
kissing the ground in front of a god or a
king.

C: Yuck.

L: Well, I'm guessing that the ground in those
days was a lot cleaner than even the church
carpet; so, let's pretend that our hands are
the ground, and if you want, you can kiss
your hand as part of your worship of Jesus.
Let's have a prayer, and we'll worship and
praise Jesus for being our Lord and King.
(Prayer)

30. He Is Not Here!

Scripture: *Luke 24:1-12*

Season/Sunday: *Easter*

Focus: *This sermon focuses on the discovery of the empty tomb, and on the words of the angels. It also looks at the difference between the reaction of the women and the men, and to some extent plays on the natural rivalry between boys and girls. Finally, it should be noted that the text from Luke 24 has several variant readings, all of which have been taken into consideration for this sermon. The reader will perhaps forgive that the sermon goes slightly farther than the text in allowing the angels to still be present when the men arrive.*

Experience: *To hear the words of the angels, first delivered to the women, then to the men.*

Arrangements: *You will need two "angels" to hide in a "tomb-like" place in the sanctuary. In its original setting this sermon employed two choir members (whose robes were an easy angelic prop), who slipped into the sacristy behind the chancel. The doorway to the sacristy became a handy entrance to the tomb, and a place for the following encounter. The angels will need to know the lines below.*

Leader:	It's great to see you this Easter morning. And what an exciting morning it is, just like that very first Easter morning. Do you remember what happened that first Easter?
Children:	Jesus arose.
L:	Indeed! And do you remember who first found out that he had risen?
C:	The disciples?

L: Yes, and specifically some of the *women* disciples. The women were the first ones to go to the tomb that morning. In fact, I have an idea: let's take you ladies right now and go around here to a place that might be kind of like where they went. You guys stay here (take girls to the "tomb"). (As you walk) So, the women went early that morning to the tomb where Jesus had been taken, and when they got there. . . .

Angel 1: "Why do you look for the living among the dead?"

Angel 2: "He is not here, but has risen!"

L: Wow! Did you hear that? What do you suppose those women did that first Easter?

Girls: Ran away?

L: Well, they ran all right, so let's get going (start "running" back to boys). They ran back to tell the men the good news (arriving where the boys are waiting): Jesus is risen!

Girls: Jesus is risen (leader should help them do this excitedly)!

L: But the men didn't take them very seriously. In fact, the Bible says that it sounded to them like "an idle tale," something that the women just made up. So they just waved the women off (help boys respond appropriately).

Boys: No way. Stop teasing. Naw.

L: But then the men started to think about it, and some of them decided to go and check for themselves. Come on, we'll all go (take boys to "tomb"), and we'll just see what happens. . . .

Angel 1: "Why do you look for the living among the dead?"

Angel 2:	"He is not here, but has risen!"
L:	(To boys) What do you suppose we should do now?
Boys:	Run away? Go and tell?
L:	Let's run and go tell the whole church: The Lord is risen! The Lord is risen!
Boys:	(running back) The Lord is risen!
All Children:	(with direction from the leader, speaking to the congregation) The Lord is risen! (Depending on your tradition, congregation may response with, "The Lord is risen indeed!")
L:	Wow! That was a lot of excitement for one morning! Let's have a prayer and thank God that Jesus Christ is risen indeed. *(Prayer)*

31. Easter Eggs

Scripture: *John 20:1-18*

Season/Sunday: *Easter*

Focus: *This sermon focuses on one of the symbols of Easter, the Easter egg, and its association with the empty tomb and new life.*

Experience: *The children will be invited to go "hunt" for some unfound Easter eggs, strangely lying in plain sight in the narthex or entry area to the church!*

Arrangements: *You will need a supply of the hinged, plastic Easter eggs typically sold at this time of year—enough to have one per child. You will also need an assistant or two to help scatter the eggs in the entry area of your church once worship has begun. Consider closing off this entry area from the* *worship space by some kind of door, so the children aren't aware of this activity. Do not hide these eggs; they should simply be lying open on the floor in plain sight. The assistants can help provide order as the children arrive to retrieve these eggs, making sure everyone takes only one and that each child gets one (a few extra eggs on hand is a wise idea!).*

Leader: Good morning! Great to see everyone on this glorious Easter day! Say, there were sure a lot of children here for the church Easter egg hunt! Did you get to be a part of that or some other Easter egg hunt?

Children: Yes. No. I found the big egg! I found a lot of eggs (and so forth).

L: Wow! Well, you know, it's the strangest thing, but I heard that there are still some eggs that weren't found, and even stranger—they're just lying out in plain sight in the narthex! Would you like to finish hunting those eggs?

C: (already on the move!) Yes!

L: Okay, but only one per person, just one egg per person! (As children return with the eggs) Let me ask you a question: Why are eggs something that we have for Easter?

C: Because of the Easter bunny?

L: I never got that: Do bunnies lay eggs?

C: No!

L: No, they don't. But that's not why we have Easter eggs. We have eggs because they remind us of birth and new life. But they also remind us of something else: the empty tomb. Like you, John and Peter ran to discover something that was empty. That tomb, like your empty eggs, had been cracked open. It burst because it was no

longer able to contain the life inside it. I'd
like you to keep these empty eggs, and I'd
like you to keep them open. Why?

C: Because of the empty tomb? As a reminder
that Jesus is risen?

L: That's exactly right. Let's have a prayer and
thank God for our Easter joy. *(Prayer)*

32. Independence Day[1]

Scripture: *Hebrews 12:1*

Season/Sunday: *Fourth of July*

Focus: *Independence Day is a great opportunity to
focus on our freedom from the bondage of sin in
Jesus Christ.*

Experience: *Children will be invited to hold a
weight out in front of them until they tire.*

Arrangements: *A box or bag filled with something
heavy. If the group is large, have several of these
"burdens" to pass around simultaneously. You may
also want one or more adult helpers to monitor this
activity while you talk.*

Leader: Good morning! Let's stay standing in a line
(or circle), and I'm going to give Brian this
heavy bag. Brian hold it out in front of you
(arms straight out assures no one will want
to hold it for too long!), and when you get
tired, you can pass it to Kelsey. You got it?

Child: (nods)

L: Great, and we'll ask my helper, Mr.
Bertelsen, to start another bag over on that
side with Steven. Great! Okay, while you're
holding and passing those heavy bags, who
can tell me what day we celebrated

1. Reprinted by permission, *Children's Ministry Magazine*, Copyright 1995,
Group Publishing, Inc., Box 481, Loveland, CO 80539.

	yesterday (or "will celebrate next Tuesday")?
Children:	Fourth of July!
L:	That's right, and sometimes we call it Independence Day. What are we independent from?
C:	Prison. Parents. England.
L:	Right, I think England is the right answer. (Check to be sure everyone is getting a chance to hold the weight.) But you know, for us as Christians, we're also free from something because of what Jesus did. Who knows what we're free from?
C:	Dying. Being bad. Our sins.
L:	All of those are good answers! And the reason we're having you pass around these heavy weights is because the letter to the Hebrews talks about sin as a weight—something heavy that we need to be free from. (Take "burdens" from children currently holding them.) Didn't it feel good, when you got tired of holding that heavy thing, to be able to pass it along? That's what Jesus has done for us: he's given us freedom from the weight of our sin, he's there to take it from us. That means that every day is Independence Day for us as Christians, if we can remember to take our sin to the cross of Jesus and not carry it around with us all the time! Let's have a prayer and ask God to help us learn how to hand over the weight of our sin to Jesus, so we can be free. *(Prayer)*

33. What a Catch!¹

Scripture: *Luke 5:1-11*

Season/Sunday: *Evangelism Sunday*

Focus: *This sermon focuses on Jesus' call to be "fishers of men (and women)." It is a fun look at the experiences of the disciples at the time Jesus issued this invitation.*

Experience: *The children (with help from the congregation) will enact the story found in Luke 5.*

Arrangements: *None are required, but if you want to enhance the experience, tape together several pieces of cardboard to create the outline of a boat (large enough to fit all the children inside). Use pieces of cardboard a foot or so wide, as long as you can find. Join them end to end and fold around to form the "sides" of a boat. (Use the same boat you made for the sermon "Walking on Water," or save the boat from this sermon to use in that one!)*

Leader: It's great to see all of you fishermen and fisherwomen today! The story we just heard was about Peter and James and John, who were on the shore one day washing out their nets. Let's pretend that the steps of the chancel are the shore, and who will be Peter and James and John? Okay, Trisha, Todd, and Sophie, and you can pretend to be washing out our nets. Good! The story says that Jesus came along and asked to use Peter's boat so he could talk to all the people on the shore. Who would like to be

---

1. My friend Randy Webb conceived this sermon. Used by permission.

Jesus? Good, Kyle. Okay, here's our boat, and Jesus you can get in, and all the rest of us will be the crowd trying to hear as Jesus speaks.

The story doesn't tell us what Jesus says, but the next thing we know, Jesus is suggesting that Simon and his partners put out their nets, the nets they had just finished cleaning, for a catch. Peter says. . . . Where's Peter? Okay Todd, Peter says . . . (coach child through these words).

Child: "Master, we have worked all night long but have caught nothing. Yet if you say so, I will let down the nets."

L: So Peter and his partners got into the boat, went out a little way (move boat down the aisle), and let down their nets. And wow! Fish were practically jumping into the boat. (To some adults nearby, "We need you to be fish—come on and jump into the boat!") And I imagine that all the people watching from the shore were amazed (encourage children on shore to show amazement— really build the excitement here).

(As boat begins to fill with "fish") And the boat started to get so full of fish that it was in danger of sinking! Did you ever fish like that?

Child: My dad did once.

L: Well, I want to meet him! Anyway, Jesus told the disciples that they would start fishing like that all the time, but not for fish. Do you know what Jesus said they would be fishing for?

C: People!

L: That's right, and our fish look a lot like

people, so we've already got a jump on that!
Let's have a prayer and thank Jesus for
inviting us to be part of this exciting way of
fishing. *(Prayer)*

34. Hip, Hip, Hooray!

Scripture: *1 Thessalonians 5:11*

Season/Sunday: *Volunteer Appreciation*

Focus: *The sermon allows the children to see and
recognize some of the servants and saints in the congregation whose work might otherwise go unnoticed.*

Experience: *The children will join in some cheers for
these volunteers.*

Arrangements: *None are needed, although you may
want to make a few notes about the people in the
church you're looking for, with extra names in mind
in case your target people aren't there. It might also
help to have the cheers written down to refer to. Feel
free to use the cheers below, to make up your own, or
even to borrow a few from the local high school team!*

Leader:	Good morning! Good to see you today. Let me ask a question: What does it mean to encourage someone?
Children:	To make them feel good, to help them, to pray for them.
L:	Those are all good answers, and I think there are some people in our church that we should encourage, because they do so many things around here that a lot of people don't notice. Let's take Don for instance (point to where person is sitting). Did you know that Don does a lot of work with the Men's

91

Breakfast Fellowship? But it's the kind of thing that most people don't get to see him do. What do you say we encourage Don with some kind of cheer. Hmmm, how about if we say, "2-4-6-8, who do we appreciate? Yea, Don!"

C: (Lead children in cheer) "2-4-6-8, who do we appreciate? Yea, Don!"

L: And then there's Ken. Did you know that Ken is the church's newsletter editor? That means he works hours and hours every month to get the church newsletter out so we can all know what's going on. I think Ken could use some encouragement. Let's see, how about, "Ken, Ken, he's our man. If he can't do it, no one can!"

C: "Ken, Ken he's our man. If he can't do it, no one can!"

L: And way back here, come on back (leading children to where the next person is sitting), way back here is Sharon. Did you know that Sharon coordinates the church prayer chain? That means that she gets phone calls at all hours of the day and night, then she calls other people, and *then* she gets down on her knees and prays for whatever it is. Wow! Let's see, it isn't really a "prayerful" cheer, but I think it might encourage her anyway if we said, "Here we go, Sharon, here we go (clap, clap). Here we go, Sharon, here we go (clap, clap). . . .

C: "Here we go, Sharon, here we go (clap, clap). Here we go, Sharon, here we go (clap, clap)."

L: Now, there are a lot of other volunteers here today, and we don't have time to encourage

them all one at a time; so what do you say
we do one last big "Hip, hip, hooray" for
everyone? Here we go.

C: "Hip, hip, hooray!"

L: That was super! And I want to encourage
and thank *you* for encouraging and thanking all our great volunteers! Let's have a
prayer and thank God that we have so
many dedicated folk who work together to
make so much happen here. *(Prayer)*

35. Love in Deed

Scripture: *1 John 3:18*

Season/Sunday: *Volunteer Appreciation*

Focus: *This sermon considers the words from 1 John
that suggest we are to love not in word or speech, but
in deed and in truth. The verse is in perfect harmony
with the primary pedagogical principle of a good children's sermon—that we communicate far more when
we go beyond words and engage in action.*

Experience: *The children will get a chance to say
"thank you" to some of the church's workers and
volunteers by telling them they are loved, and then
showing them that they are loved.*

Arrangements: *None are needed, except to think
through which volunteer groups you will want to
call out.*

Leader: Good morning! It is great to see you, and
we've got a lot to do! But first, let me ask
you, is it good to tell people we love them?

Children: Yes!

L: Well, of course it is! And so this morning we

C: need to tell some people we love them. I'm
going to call out some of the church's volunteers, and let me just say at the start that this
is only a partial list! Now when they stand
up, let's all say a big "We love you." Ready?

C: Yes!

L: Okay, let's start with all of our Scout leaders. If you are a Scout leader of whatever
kind, or you have been, or you are in
another church or school, would you please
stand? (Leaders stand.) Okay, ready, one,
two, three. . . .

C: We love you!

L: Great! Okay Scouts, you can be seated.
Now, if you are a tutor in our literacy program, or have been in the past, or tutor in
any other capacity, would you please stand?
(Tutors stand.) Okay, ready?

C: We love you!

L: Thank you tutors, and you can be seated.
Okay, now let's thank the drivers and others
who help with the meals program. If you've
ever been involved with the meals program,
would you please stand? (Volunteers stand.)
Here we go. . . .

C: We love you!

L: And you may be seated. (To children) Well,
that was nice, but now, let me ask you, was
that enough?

C: Yes. No. You didn't tell my mommy.

L: I'm sure we didn't get to everyone we
needed to, but even more than that, the
Bible says that we are not only to love with
our words, but also with our deeds.
Hmmm. How could we love all of these volunteers with our deeds?

C: Give them something.

L: Okay, what do we have to give them (prompt with motions indicating a hug or a handshake)?

C: A hug! A handshake!

L: What great ideas, or maybe even a high five! In just a minute I'll ask all of those people to stand again, and on your way back to your seat you can give two or three of them a hug, a handshake, or a high five. But first, let's have a prayer and thank God that there are so many people who want to serve, and that we can love them in word and in deed. *(Prayer)* (Ask volunteers to stand as children are dismissed.)

36. Serving Two Masters

Scripture: *Matthew 6:24*

Season/Sunday: *Stewardship*

Focus: *Many things compete for "leadership" in our lives, even in the lives of children. This sermon focuses on how the "leadership competition" can be confusing.*

Experience: *The children will play "Follow the Leader," but with a twist: there will be two leaders!*

Arrangements: *Early in the week ask another adult to be the second leader. Share a copy of the script, and perhaps even get together to practice.*

Leader 1:   Good morning! Today we're going to play "Follow the Leader." Have you ever played this game?

Children: Yes!

L: Good, then you know that all you need to do is what the leader says. But this game will be a little different, because we're going to have two leaders! That should make it twice as fun! Okay, everybody on their feet and let's do some jumping jacks—that's it, follow the leader!

Leader 2: (oblivious to Leader 1) Okay, everybody stand still. That's right, stand still.

L1: (oblivious to L2) Jump! Everybody do jumping jacks.

L2: Good. Now that you're standing still, I want you to rub your tummy and pat your head.

L1: Okay, now that we're done with jumping jacks lets all give one another a hug. Come on everyone give a hug and get a hug.

L2: That's right, keep rubbing your tummy and patting your head.

L1: (as children complain more and more) What? You mean you can't follow two leaders? No! And that's what Jesus said, too. He said, "No one can serve two masters; for a slave will either hate the one and love the other, or be devoted to the one and despise the other. You cannot serve God and wealth." Jesus is saying that if we try to serve two masters, we'll end up hating one or the other. In this case Jesus was talking about God and money. Can you think of some ways that money is a master, or a leader, to people?

Children: It can make a person greedy; it can make you selfish.

L2: Right, and those aren't good things. On the other hand, what would God tell us to do with our money?

C: Use it to help people, give it away.

L1:   Right again, and in that way God is the real
        master, and money just gets used to do good
        things that God leads us to. Let's have a
        prayer and thank God that we only need to
        serve one master. *(Prayer)*

37. Ten Tenths

Scripture: *Malachi 3:10, Ephesians 4:11*

Season/Sunday: *Stewardship*

Focus: *This sermon demonstrates the twin concepts
of* tithing *(returning to God one-tenth of all God has
given to us) and* gifting *(the idea that God has gifted
the church for ministry). The unifying theme of these
two ideas is a* stewardship *that seeks to recognize
and return to God a tenth of the gifts God has given.*

Experience: *Children and adults will be asked to get
into groups of ten. Out of each group, different gifts
and skills will be called for, including one or two
that only a child will have.*

Arrangements: *None are needed, but be sure to give
some thought to how you will divide the congregation into groups of ten. If there are more than a couple of hundred people present, this division will, at
the very least, take slightly longer.*

Leader: Good morning! Children, I don't want you
            to come forward this morning, but instead, I
            want you to stand up with nine other people
            around you. Congregation, that means you
            get to play, too! We're trying to establish
            groups of ten by simply standing where you
            are and looking group-like. Try to have at

least one child in every group if you can, although that's not critical. Some of us may have to move around a little—that's it. Good!

Okay, today we're looking at the gifts God gives to the church. The Bible tells us that God has provided the church with everything it needs to do the job Jesus has given us to do—to make disciples. The Bible also tells us that all of us are to return a portion of our time, treasure, and talent back to God. We call this portion a tithe, 10 percent of all that we have. So, being in groups of ten we're going to find the 10 percent of each of your groups that have the following gifts. Ready? Remember, each person can only be chosen once!

If God needed someone from your group who was the shortest, to pick the prettiest flowers, who would that person be? (Give group time to identify that person.) So that person is your group's tithe of finding beauty.

If God needed someone from your group who was the oldest, to give wisdom, who would that be? (Give group time to identify that person.) Okay, so that person is your group's tithe of wisdom.

If God needed someone from your group who was the tallest, to see the way ahead, who would that be? (Give group time to identify that person.) That person is your group's tithe of tallness.

If God needed someone from your group who was good at teaching, to teach somewhere in the life of the church, who would that be? (Give group time to identify that person.) So that person is your group's tithe of teaching.

If God needed someone from your group who was musical, to sing in the choir, who would that be? (Give group time to identify that person.) Okay, so that person is your group's tithe of singing.

If God needed someone from your group who was a gardener, to pull the weeds around the church, who would that person be? (Give group time to identify that person.) That person is your group's tithe of yard work.

If God needed someone from your group who was good with children, to take care of children, who would that person be? (Give group time to identify that person.) Okay, so that person is your group's tithe of child care.

If God needed someone from your group to be the quietest, to listen to someone's hurts, who would that person be? (Give group time to identify that person.) That person is your group's tithe of caring.

If God needed someone from your group to be the "huggingest," to give the best hugs, who would that person be? (Give group time to identify that person.) So that person is your group's tithe of hugs!

And finally, if God needed someone from your group with the best smile, to brighten our day, who would that person be? And that person is your group's tithe of smiles.

Isn't it great that God gives so many gifts! Let's have prayer and give thanks that we are so gifted as a church, and that God invites us to return a part of our gifts as our way of giving thanks. *(Prayer)*

38. Thank You!

Scripture: *Luke 17:11-19*

Season/Sunday: *Thanksgiving*

Focus: *In our fast-paced culture, sometimes we don't say "thanks" enough. And that, of course, is the whole point of the Thanksgiving holiday!*

Experience: *The children will be able to say "thanks."*

Arrangements: *None.*

Leader:	Good morning. Say, let me ask you a question: when do you say thanks to people?
Children:	When they do something nice for me. When they give me something. When they take care of my cat.
L:	Okay, and do you think you say enough thanks? I mean, when was the last time you said thanks to your parents, your Sunday school teacher, or even to God?
C:	Today. Yesterday. Never.
L:	Okay, I have an idea. Will all the teachers and officers of the church please stand (include any others you'd like to have thanked). Okay, let's all go and find one of these people and say five "thank yous" to them. As soon as you finish, that person can sit down and you can go on to the next one. Go!
	(As all of these people sit down) Good! Okay, go find your parents and say ten

"thank yous" to them, then come on back up here.

(As children re-gather). That was great. I hope you'll remember to keep up the thanks-giving during Thanksgiving. Let's have a prayer and let's say *fifty* "thank yous" to God (about one minute). *("Thank you" prayer)*

39. King Jesus Is All

Scripture: *Psalm 22:3*

Season/Sunday: *Christ the King (last Sunday before Advent)*

Focus: *This sermon focuses on the intriguing idea that God's throne consists of our praise. That's what Psalm 22:3 tells us, "God is enthroned on the praises of Israel." Thus when we praise we build up God's throne!*

Experience: *Children will experience a contemporary practice of "enthroning," and then experience the biblical practice of enthroning.*

Arrangements: *Identify and contact two or three strong young teens or adults early in the week, to verify that they will be present on Sunday, and that their backs are in fairly good shape! (Together they only have to lift one small child.)*

Leader:	Good morning! Great to see everyone! The first thing we need this morning is a volunteer to be a "coach." Any volunteers? Okay, Ian, you are our coach. Great, now, what do they do to coaches after the team wins?
Children:	They throw ice on them!

L: That's right, and we have a bucket right here—*just kidding*! Okay, what else do teams do to coaches when they win?

C: Put the coach up on their shoulders.

L: That's right, the team makes the coach a kind of king, or queen, and carries him or her around on the throne of their shoulders. And that *is* what we're going to do with Coach Ian! (Volunteers put child on their shoulders.) And then the team cheers (lead cheer, and a short victory parade around the area).

C: Hip, hip, hooray!

L: (having gotten child "coach" safely down) Who is our King?

C: Jesus. God.

L: That's right, and can we put Jesus up on our shoulders to make a throne and celebrate all he has done for us?

C: No!

L: What could we do? Oh, I know, let's look in the Bible. It says in Psalm 22 that our King is "enthroned" on our praises. What does "enthroned" mean?

C: (may or may not know)

L: Well, it means that our praise and worship are the throne of Jesus. So how do we praise and worship Jesus?

C: Sing?

L: That's right, we can sing. Let's all sing out "Hallelujah" (lead one word from Handel's *Messiah*).

C: "Hallelujah!"

L: What else? Could we say "Praise the Lord"? Let's try that.

C: "Praise the Lord!"

L: Or how about "Glory!" (By now the con-
    gregation should be encouraged to partici-
    pate if they're not already!)
C: "Glory!"
L: Everything we do in worship together is
    part of making a throne for King Jesus. Let's
    hold hands and have a prayer and give
    thanks that we're able to praise King Jesus
    this way. *(Prayer)*

Sacraments

40. Go, Make, Baptize, Teach

Scripture: *Matthew 28:18-20*

Season/Sunday: *Baptism (could also be used on an Evangelism Sunday)*

Focus: *This sermon focuses on the four verbs in the Great Commission:* go, make, baptize, *and* teach.

Experience: *The children will be invited to enact these four verbs in ways that will encourage their understanding of the* active *nature of our work as Christians.*

Arrangements: *None.*

Leader: Good morning! Say, this is a special day in the life of the church because we're going to baptize Austin, Taylor, and Haley. But did you know that baptizing people is only part of what Jesus commanded us to do? Listen to what Jesus says in Matthew 28, and see if you can hear the four things Jesus tells us we should be doing: "All authority in heaven and on earth has been given to me. Go therefore and make disciples of all

	nations, baptizing them in the name of the Father and of the Son and of the Holy Spirit, and teaching them to obey everything that I have commanded you. And remember, I am with you always, to the end of the age." Did you hear the four things?
Children:	Authority? Baptize? Go? Jesus loves me?
L:	All of those are good answers, and we've got some of the four things. Jesus told us to go to people, to make disciples of them, to baptize them, and to teach them. Hmm, I wonder if we should try that right now? Everybody up! Look out there at that congregation. Someone out there needs you to *go* to them (leader should extend one arm forward, hand open). Go find someone out there and have them stand up with you in the aisle (as children disperse, leader should remain standing with arm extended).
C:	(find someone in the congregation)
L:	Okay, Jesus told us to "go," and we went. Next he tells us to "make disciples." I think the best way to do that is to pray for someone. So put your hands together and both of you bow your heads, as if you were praying (leader follows suit by bending arm and assuming a posture of prayer with hands together).
C:	(put hands together)
L:	Great! Then Jesus says we are to baptize, so if possible, adults would you kneel, and children, put your hand on the head of the adult in front of you, like you are baptizing them.
C:	(put hand on head of adult)
L:	Super! Now the last thing Jesus told us to

do was to teach, so for this, why don't we put our hands together as if they were an open book (leader should show this motion).

C: (put hands together)
L: That was really good. Adults, you can stand up now, and then let's all go through these four motions one more time, congregation you can join us. *Go* (arm forward, with hand open), *make disciples* (hands together in prayer), *baptize* (hand outstretched, palm down), and *teach* (hands together as a book). Wonderful. Let's have a prayer and thank God for this great commission. *(Prayer)*

41. Dizzy!

Scripture: *Luke 3:1-14 (or any other of the many "repent" texts in the Bible)*

Season/Sunday: *Baptism*

Focus: *This sermon describes the nature of repentance as a complete change of course, and shows how God's grace stabilizes us in our dizzying cycle of repentance.*

Experience: *The children will turn around and around and around!*

Arrangements: *None.*

Leader: Good morning! Does anyone know what the word "repent" means?
Children: To stop doing something bad. To be sorry.
L: That's right, it means to stop doing something, to be sorry, to change. It means all of

those things, and the way the Bible uses the word it means "to turn around." Everybody stand up. Spread out so you have a little room. Okay, now let's all face this way (indicate a direction) and pretend we're doing something wrong. The Bible says we should repent, which means that we should turn around (everyone should turn around). Good! Okay, but now what happens if we sin again?

C: Turn around again!
L: That's right (turn back around). Sin again?
C: Turn around (turning around)!
L: Sin.
C: Turn around.
L: Sin.
C: Turn around.
L: I'm *dizzy!* Wow! I don't know about you, but all the sinning and repenting I do in my life leaves me a little dizzy! We need something to stop all this turning and turning and turning. Baptism does that for us. We can put our hand on our head (demonstrate and encourage participation) and remember that we have been baptized, cleansed, and claimed by God. That hand on our head can help hold us steady! Let's have a prayer and thank God for helping us not be so dizzy with sin. (*Prayer*)

42. Rooted and Grounded

Scripture: *Ephesians 3:14-21*

Season/Sunday: *Baptism*

Focus: *In the text Paul prays that God's people,*

"being rooted and grounded in love, may have power to comprehend with all the saints" the love of God. This sermon describes how that rooting and grounding take place in and through the community.

Experience: *The children will experience being like trees (an apt metaphor for discipleship—see Psalm 1), and will be "rooted and grounded" by adult helpers.*

Arrangements: *None.*

Leader:	Good morning, I'd like to invite all the children to come forward with a parent or other loving adult. We need one adult per child, so let me invite a few extra adults forward, too (oversee this one-to-one arrangement as quickly as possible). Great! Now, let me ask all of the children to pretend that you are a tree. How would you be a tree?
Children:	Put our arms up.
L:	Right, put your arms up, put your legs together to be the trunk, maybe put your fingers out to be leaves. Those are some good lookin' trees! Now, let's pretend that you are blowing in the wind of the Spirit, in order to know the breadth and length and height and depth of the love of Christ. That means we need to gently sway as far as you can, forward and backward, side to side, even up and down, reaching to know Christ's love. Great! So, could you reach very far?
C:	Yes, no.
L:	Do you think you could reach even further if somebody helped to "root and ground" you? Let's ask all of the adults to get down

on the floor, or at least as close to it as you can, and hold your child around the knees. Good, and children, now that you're rooted and grounded, let's try gently swaying forward and back, and side to side, and see if you can go further than you did before.

C: Yes!

L: Well, that's exactly how it's supposed to work! When we baptize someone in the church, all of the adults are coming around that person and promising to help root and ground them, so that they can reach farther and farther, and explore more and more the love of Christ. Let's have a prayer and thank God for those who love us, and for the love of Christ that surpasses knowledge, and for the church that roots and grounds us. *(Prayer)*

43. The Imitation of Christ

Scripture: *Luke 22:17-23 (also Mark 1:35, Luke 6:12, Matthew 8:15, Matthew 20:34)*

Season/Sunday: *Lord's Supper*

Focus: *This sermon focuses on being recognized as a follower of Jesus because we share the same habits he had: pious prayer, tender touch, and holy hospitality.*

Experience: *After talking about how we recognize people by their habits, the children will learn some of the habits of Jesus.*

Arrangements: *None are needed. However, if you have some high profile people in the congregation who can take a little kidding (clear it with them first!) you might try to think of some of their* *particular habits or mannerisms to use as examples with the children.*

Leader: Good to see you today. Let's all stand because we're going to need some room to do some things here. Okay, when you see this (pretend to stroke a beard and invite everyone to join in imitating), who does it remind you of?

Children: My dad! You! Mr. Bloom.

L: Good! What if you see someone doing this, (pretend to fix hair and invite everyone to join in imitating), who does it remind you of?

C: My mom! My sister! A girl at school! Amy!

L: Okay, one more. When you see someone doing this (suck your teeth while pulling your earlobes or make some other mildly disgusting gesture and invite everyone to imitate), who does it remind you of?

C: No one!

L: I was hoping you'd say that! Well, it's true, isn't it, that we can recognize some people by their habits?

C: Yes.

L: And it's also true, isn't it, that if we really admire someone, if we really like them and look up to them, that we might try and copy some of their habits?

C: Yes. My little sister is always copying me.

L: Exactly! Little brothers and sisters often copy their big brothers and sisters because they look up to them and want to be just like them. Well, if I were to fold my hands like this (fold hands in prayer, invite children to imitate), who would that remind you of?

C: The minister. My grandmother. Jesus.

L: Good answers, and I think Jesus is the one we're looking for, because all people who follow Jesus want to do what he did, which is to make it a habit to pray. The Bible tells us that Jesus was in the habit of praying, sometimes getting up early in the morning, sometimes praying all night (Mark 1:35, Luke 6:12). Good! Okay, what if I were to reach out and gently touch Kelly on the shoulder, or come alongside Joshua here and give him a hug (invite children to engage in similar tender touch), would that also remind you of Jesus?

C: Yes.

L: And that's because we have lots of stories about Jesus tenderly touching people around him, to love them, to heal them, and to care for them (Matthew 8:15, Matthew 20:34). Okay, one last one: what if you saw me (or whoever is appropriate could at this point move behind the Communion table) break this bread, who would it remind you of?

C: Jesus.

L: That's right, because this is what Jesus did the night before he was put on the cross. And whenever we practice the habit of breaking bread together people will recognize us as followers of Jesus, too. Let's have a prayer and thank God for these many ways we can imitate Jesus. *(Prayer)*

44. The Emmaus Road

Scripture: *Luke 24:13-35*

Season/Sunday: *Lord's Supper*

Focus: *This sermon focuses on the wonderful story of the two disciples on the road to Emmaus, and by extension, the way our own eyes can be opened to the presence of Christ when we gather at the Table.*

Experience: *The children will be invited to go on a walk around the sanctuary, remembering some of the events surrounding Jesus' death and resurrection.*

Arrangements: *None are needed, but consider beforehand the route for the "journey" you want to take, and what you will say.*

Leader:	Good morning, we're going on a journey today (start walking) while we pretend to be the two disciples we just heard about in the Bible reading. Do you remember the story? The two men were walking from Jerusalem to a village called Emmaus. It was a special day, Easter Sunday, but they didn't know it yet. In fact, do you remember, were they happy or sad?
Children:	Sad.
L:	That's right, so let's pretend that we are them, and we are walking to Emmaus and that we are sad. Why were they sad?
C:	Because Jesus had died.
L:	That's right, and they didn't know yet that he had risen. But then someone joined them on the road, do you know who it was?
C:	Jesus.

L: It *was* Jesus, but did the two men recognize him?

C: No!

L: No, they didn't. Can you imagine right now that someone is joining us? We'll pretend that Jesus is joining us on our walk, but that we don't recognize him. The two disciples talked to him while they walked, and told him all about what had happened, and they listened to him tell about scripture, too.

(As the group arrives at the Communion table) Finally, they arrived at the place where they were staying, and the men said to Jesus, "Stay with us." And as they sat down to their evening meal, the scripture says that Jesus took the bread, and blessed it, and broke it, and gave it to them, and do you know what happened next?

C: They recognized him!

L: That's right—they recognized him. And as soon as they recognized him, what happened?

C: They were happy!

L: They *were* happy, but the other thing that happened is that Jesus vanished from their sight, and they were so excited that they decided to run back to Jerusalem to tell all of their friends (start running, or at least walking fast, back along the way that you came, talking excitedly and with energy!). And when they got back (even if you're not "back" yet), they announced to all the disciples, "The Lord is risen!" (Lead children to excitedly announce this to the congregation, as you continue to make your way back.)

C: The Lord is risen! The Lord is risen!

L: (still excitedly) And when they told that to the other disciples, they found out that everyone already knew, they said, "The Lord is risen, indeed!" (Lead congregation to make this traditional response to the announcement of the children.)

Wow! That was so exciting that I'm out of breath! Let's have a prayer and thank God that our Lord Jesus Christ is risen indeed. *(Prayer)*

45. One Loaf

Scripture: *1 Corinthians 11:17-34*

Season/Sunday: *Lord's Supper*

Focus: *This sermon focuses on our equality at the Lord's table as children of God. We partake of "one loaf" because we are "one people" before God.*

Experience: *The children will watch different groups of people receive different kinds of elements, in a way associated with communion.*

Arrangements: *You will need a number of youth and adults to assist with this message. Depending on the dynamics of your church, you can invite them ahead of time, or simply "grab" them out of the congregation when the time comes (they have minimal duties).*

Prepare a platter that contains some cookies (with the exact number of adults you plan to have come forward), some cubes of bread (with the exact number of teens you plan to have come forward), and some torn squares of cardboard (enough for the children who normally come forward). Cover the platter and place it on Communion table along with the elements for the day's Communion.

Leader: Good morning. I'm going to ask my youth and adult helpers to come forward right now, too. This is a special day in worship because we have a special celebration. (Remove cover from platter, making sure everyone can see all that's on it. Hand each adult a cookie, each youth a piece of bread, and each child a piece of cardboard. Don't let them serve themselves, and start with the adults and youth so that cardboard is all that's left for the children. In the meantime, talk about how special the celebration of the Lord's Supper is. When you finish serving ask . . .) Everybody happy?

Children: No!

L: Why not?

C: We want a cookie. We just got this piece of cardboard. It's not fair!

L: You know, you're right, it's not fair because it's not all the same. Is this the way we celebrate the Lord's Supper?

C: No!

L: How do we celebrate communion? (Hold up loaf or paten with bread/wafers.)

C: We all get the same.

L: We do all get the same. Why is that?

C: Because we're all the same to God. Because we're all children of God.

L: That's right, and aren't we glad that when we receive communion later in the service we'll all receive a piece of bread. Let's hold hands and have a prayer and give thanks that God treats us all the same, young and old alike, and that we are all one before our Lord. *(Prayer)*

46. Neither Greek nor Jew

Scripture: *Colossians 3:11-17*

Season/Sunday: *Lord's Supper*

Focus: *This sermon focuses on labels—those we put on ourselves and those put on us by others. The sermon points out that only one label counts when we come to the Lord's table, the label placed on us by God.*

Experience: *The children will reflect on the practice of "labeling" and then be labeled "One for whom Christ died," as part of their preparation for Communion.*

Arrangements: *You will need enough printed labels (the kind used for most church mailings will work just fine) for each child to have one. Each label should say, "One for whom Christ died." In addition, you will need three or four labels with words or phrases that describe yourself.*

Leader: Good morning! Let's gather in a big circle around the Communion table. That's great!

Say, I have a question for you, have you ever heard anyone put a label on someone else? A label is a quick way of talking about someone else, and is supposed to describe that person. For example, some people put a label on me (placing label on self) that says "Preacher." To some people that means they have to be real good when they think I'm watching, even if they're not really good other times when only God is watching. Another label people sometimes put on me (sticking on another label) says "Red

116

	Head." To some people that means I might have a temper. Another label people sometimes put on me says "Californian," and that's, like, fer sure, supposed to mean, like, I don't know.
	Can you think of some labels that we sometimes put on other people?
Children:	(may or may not come up with any)
L:	Some that I thought of are labels like "bully," "sissy," or "skater," or even "black" or "white" or "rich" or "poor."
	Well, let me ask you this: what label do we need to come to this Table and receive the Lord's Supper?
C:	None. Christian.
L:	(Hand out labels for children to stick on themselves.) The only label we need is the one that says we are "One for whom Christ died." These labels could also say, "Christian" or "disciple" or lots of other things. But all of those mean the same thing—that we're forgiven, and that we're someone who is seeking to know and follow Christ. That's why, a little while later in the service, you'll hear me say, "All who call on the name of Christ are welcome, all people for whom Christ died." Let's have a prayer and give thanks that there's only one label that matters to God. *(Prayer)*

Mother's and Father's Day

47. Mama, Do You Love Me?

Scripture: *Hosea 14:1-9*

Season/Sunday: *Mother's Day*

Focus: *The main theme of the book of Hosea is the never-exhausted love of God, even when God's people stray. The allegory for delivering this message was that Hosea married a prostitute named Gomer, whom he would love despite her unfaithfulness. This is probably not someplace you want to go with young children on a Sunday morning, but another allegory they might better relate to comes from the delightful children's book,* Mama, Do You Love Me? *by Barbara M. Joosse. The book is set in the Inuit culture, and the sermon below is indebted to its inspiration.*

Experience: *The leader will ask parents to affirm their never-exhausted love for their children in various hypothetical situations.*

Arrangements: *Make a list of hypothetical questions.*

Leader: Good morning, it's great to see everyone. Hey, I have a question for you: Do your parents love you?

Children:	Yes, usually, no, sometimes.
L:	Well most of you said yes, and I'm willing to bet that your parents do love you, so why don't we go ask them. (To a child) Where are your parents? (Child points.) Well, let's all go over there. Good morning!
Parents:	Good morning.
L:	So, do you love Brittney?
P:	We do!
L:	Okay, well, that's good, but now, let me ask you, what if Brittney was carrying the groceries in from the car next Saturday, and she tried to be careful, and walked slowly, but she fell, and all the eggs broke—would you still love her?
P:	Yes, we'd still love her!
L:	Great. Okay, who else? John, where is your mom? Let's all go visit John's mom. Good morning!
P:	Good morning!
L:	So, do you love John?
P:	Yes, I do, very much.
L:	Well, okay, but not so fast! What if John put spam in your jacket, and hamsters in your gloves, and mice in your shoes? Not that he would, but if he did, would you still love him?
P:	Yes. I might be upset, but I'd still love him.
L:	Well all right then, who else? Katie, where are your grandparents? Let's all go visit Katie's grandparents. Hello, do you love Katie?
Grandparents:	Yes, we do!
L:	Easy to say. But what if Katie took all the good lightbulbs out of the lamps and replaced them with burned out lightbulbs, huh? Then what?

GP: Well, I guess we'd be in the dark, but we'd still let our love shine.

L: Wow, good answer! Okay, one more. Let's see, okay, how about you Joseph? Where's your dad? Let's all go visit Joseph's dad. So, Dad, inquiring minds want to know, do you love Joseph?

P: I do.

L: Like we haven't heard *that* before. Okay, but what if—let's make this good—what if Joseph ran away and moved in with the coyotes, and howled at the moon, and ate yucky stuff so that he had bad breath.

P: Well, I would miss him, and I'd hope that he'd come back soon, and maybe that he would brush his teeth, but yes, I'd still love him.

L: (To children) You know, as much as your parents love you, even when you might not always do the right thing, do you know that God loves you even more? The Bible is full of stories, like one in Hosea, about how God keeps loving us, and looking for us, and coming to find us, no matter what kinds of messes we get ourselves into. Let's have a prayer and say thanks for that amazing love. *(Prayer)*

48. A Good Wife, Who Can Find?

Scripture: *Proverbs 31:10-31*

Season/Sunday: *Mother's Day*

Focus: *This sermon focuses on the biblical description of a good wife (which includes no mention of children until the end!). The leader is encouraged to*

*be sensitive to those for whom Mother's Day is not
an occasion for celebration (those whose children
have died, those experiencing infertility, and so
forth).*

Experience: *The children will hear the biblical
description of a good wife and respond accordingly.*

Arrangements: *None.*

Leader:	Good morning, I bet you know what day it is today!
Children:	Mother's Day!
L:	That's right, and in honor of this special day I thought I'd read you a description of what a good wife and mother is according to the book of Proverbs. It starts with the question, "A good wife who can find?" Hmmm. While I keep reading this, why don't you go out and try to find a good wife? It might be your mother, or it might be somebody you just think might make a good wife, and once you've found that person, bring them back up here. (As children leave to find this person continue reading from Proverbs 31:10-28. By then everyone should be gathered back at the front.)

(Finishing verse 27) Now in verse 28 it says, "Her children rise up and call her blessed . . ." (RSV). So children, turn to the woman you brought up here, and on the count of three, say "Blessed!" Ready? One, two, three, "Blessed!" Good. Then it says, "Her husband also, and he praises her, 'Many women have done excellently, but you surpass them all' " (RSV). So men, if you're married to one of these good wives up here, would you stand up and repeat after me. (Give the men a few words at a time to repeat back.) Perfect! Let's have a prayer and thank God for great wives and mothers. *(Prayer)*

49. Honor Your Mother[1]

Scripture: *Ephesians 6:1-3*

Season/Sunday: *Mother's Day (could also be used for Father's Day)*

Focus: *The sermon focuses on possible meanings and behaviors associated with the word "honor."*

Experience: *The children will be asked to reflect on the word "honor." They will then experience four ways to express this concept.*

Arrangements: *None are needed, but a constant issue in sermons such as these is sensitivity to children whose mother or father may not be present. Always be sure to invite a substitute parent or parental figure.*

Leader:	Good morning! Let me invite all of the children to come forward and to bring their mother or another woman you know. Fathers are allowed to substitute! So, the Bible says we're supposed to "honor" our mothers (or fathers). What does that word mean? What does it mean to "honor" someone?
Children:	To respect them?
L:	Sure, that's one of the meanings. Okay, so how could we show our mothers respect?

1. My thanks to Catherine Bloom for help with the original idea for this children's sermon.

C: By bowing? (Suggest this if no children come up with it or something else suitable, and so on throughout.)

L: What a great idea! Let's all bow to our mothers.

C: (bow)

L: Okay, so what else does it mean to honor someone?

C: (They may be out of ideas!)

L: Does it maybe also mean to obey?

C: (nods)

L: And how could we show our moms right now that we obey them? How about a salute?

C: (children salute moms)

L: Okay, now I looked this up and to honor someone can also mean to thank them. Let's see, how could we show thanks?

C: Say "thank you"?

L: That's right, and while we do, let's also applaud (begin clapping). Good, now say "thank you."

C: Thank you!

L: Okay, to honor means to respect (bow), to obey (salute), to thank (applaud), and finally, it means to love. How about if we show that by giving a hug?

C: (give hugs)

L: Hey, I've got a great idea, let's do all four of those in a row! Ready, here we go . . .

C: (Bow, salute, applaud while saying, "thank you," and then give a hug. Feel free to do it more than once if everyone's having fun!)

L: That was great! Let's have a prayer and thank God for giving us moms and other people who love us so much that we want to honor them. *(Prayer)*

50. Choose This Day Whom You Will Serve

Scripture: *Joshua 23:1-13, 24:14-15*

Season/Sunday: *Father's Day*

Focus: *The sermon focuses on making choices—specifically, how father figures in our lives help guide the choices we make.*

Experience: *The children will be given a choice about leaving church during worship.*

Arrangements: *The week before, contact two or three "empty nest" fathers (men whose children have grown up and left home). Ask them to assist you by quietly taking posts at the doors of the church during the time when the children come forward. Their job, in the unlikely event that it needs to be done, is to help guide (and change!) the choice of any child who might decide to leave during the children's sermon.*

Leader:	Good morning! Can I have all the children come forward? It's great to see you all. I want to ask you this morning about choices. Do you have any choices to make in your life, any decisions that you have to make during the day? What are some of them?
Children:	What game to play at school on the playground. What to have for lunch in the cafeteria. What to watch on television. What answers to give on a test.
L:	Those are all good answers, and of course, there are lots more that we could mention, like whether we'll be nice or mean when we play, and whether we'll be thankful or not

for our food, and whether we'll watch good shows or shows we know we shouldn't watch on television, and whether we'll take our test honestly or cheat. There are lots and lots of choices!

Well now, let me ask you this: Are you ever guided in your choices and decisions by your father's (or mother's) decision? Or by the decisions of other important adults in your life?

C: Yes. No. Sometimes.

L: Well, let's just try a little test. I'm going to give you a choice to make right now. You can choose to leave church right now, or you can choose to stay. What do you choose?

C: (Some look like they might go; most shake head; and in the end all stay.)

L: You made a good choice, and I think that you might have been helped by knowing your father (or mother) would choose for you to stay. But I'll tell you a little secret: just in case any of you had made a different choice, I asked some other fathers to stand at the doors to help you with that choice! Those fathers all have grown up children, but they know that they're still responsible to be fathers to you. Let's have a prayer and thank God that our church is like that, a place where we have lots of fathers, and mothers, and grandparents, and uncles, and aunts, and all kinds of people who love us, to help us with our choices. *(Prayer)*

51. A Father's Voice

Scripture: *Psalm 95:7*

Season/Sunday: *Father's Day*

Focus: *This sermon focuses on listening to our fathers' voices to guide and lead us.*

Experience: *Children will listen for the voice of their father (or mother) with their eyes closed.*

Arrangements: *None.*

Leader:	Good morning! I'd like to ask the children to come forward with your father, or another adult whose voice you know. Well, it's Father's Day and I thought we'd play a little game, but first let me ask you, do you listen to your father's voice (use language inclusive of other adults children brought, if necessary, here and throughout)?
Children:	Yes!
L:	Always? Well, we'll see how well you can hear your father's voice. Everybody stand up (if sitting), and separate from your father. That's right, drift apart and just mingle around in the group. Okay, children, close your eyes. Now dads, in just a minute I'll ask you to call your child, or children, to you by name. Children, you need to move slowly and carefully to your dads, keeping your eyes closed until you are there. Everybody got it? Okay dads, go ahead.
Dads:	(call out for children)
L:	(When everyone is "found") Good, now that you have the hang of it, we're going to do it again, except this time the dads aren't allowed

to call your name. They're just going to talk—about what a beautiful day it is, about how their favorite team is playing, about what they have planned for the rest of the day—and you have to find them, still with your eyes closed, just by listening to their voice. Ready? Let's mingle around, separate a little ways. Good—mingle, mingle. Okay, children close your eyes; dads start talking.

Dads: (talk)

L: (When everyone is found) That was great! Do you think that game would have been harder if you didn't know your father's or loved one's voice? What if we had a complete stranger up here, talking about the price of wheat, and you had to pick out their voice—could you do it?

C: No! Maybe. Depends.

L: Well you know, it's got to be easier to follow your dad's directions if you know the sound of his voice. And that's true with God, too. The Bible tells us that we're to listen to God's voice and follow where God leads. Let's have a prayer and thank God that we have so many good voices calling out and guiding us. *(Prayer)*

52. Still Working

Scripture: *John 5:17*

Season/Sunday: *Father's Day*

Focus: *While somewhat abstract, the focus of this sermon is on ways we can be "at work," just as the Father is at work. In this case, the "work" in question is prayer.*

Experience: *The children will follow the lead of a father from the church in his work of prayer.*

Arrangements: *You will need to arrange for a father to be in the narthex (or outside, if your church lacks an enclosed narthex space). This father's assignment is to walk back and forth, saying the Lord's Prayer (normal voice, continuously repeating). The narthex, or main, doors should be closed.*

Leader:	Good morning! How is everyone today?
Children:	Good! Fine!
L:	That's great! Say, I wonder if you can see through the windows in the doors back there and notice that Mr. Alexander is walking around in the narthex. Not only that, he's showing us and telling us something that he wants us to do, too. So, let's all do it.
C:	What? We can't.
L:	You can't? Why not?
C:	We can't see/hear him!
L:	Hmm. That is a problem. Maybe if we moved a little closer? Let's try that (rising and moving about half way toward the doors). Okay? Go!
C:	Nooo! We still can't see/hear him!
L:	Oh, darn. Well, what can we do?
C:	Go all the way, move closer.
L:	Okay, well, if you think that's how to do it. Let me understand, we want to move closer to this father, so we can watch him and listen to what he's doing. Is that right?
C:	Right, let's go! (Go to narthex doors, open, and listen.)
L:	So, what is he doing?

C: Saying the Lord's Prayer.

L: That's right, and he's walking around, kind of spreading it around. Say, you don't suppose Mr. Alexander is trying to tell us something about God, too? Jesus told us that *his* Father was still working, and so Jesus was working, too. And Mr. Alexander is Stephen's father, and he is working by walking around and praying, and he wants us to be at work, too. And the only way we could know what he was doing was by getting closer to him, just like we can only know what God is doing by getting closer to God, and, and—wow! That's a lot of stuff, but, do you think it's all true?!

C: Yes!

L: Well, then, let's do it! Thanks Mr. Alexander, for giving us that example! Let's walk back up toward the front of the church and, as we walk, say the Lord's Prayer for our closing prayer. *(Prayer)*

Bibliography

Bailey, Kenneth E. *Poet and Peasant*. Grand Rapids: William B. Eerdmans Publishing, 1976.

Bainton, Roland. *Christendom*. New York: Harper Torchbooks, 1964.

Barclay, William. *The Gospel of John*, vol 2. Philadelphia: The Westminster Press, 1975.

Berryman, Jerome W. *Godly Play: A Way of Religious Education*. San Francisco: HarperSanFrancisco, 1991.

Joosse, Barbara M. *Mama, Do You Love Me?* Illustrated by Barbara Lavalle. San Francisco: Chronicle Books, 1991.

Miller, David L. *Gods and Games*. New York: The World Publishing Company, 1969.

Moltmann, Jürgen. *Theology of Play*. Translated by Reinhard Ulrich. Harper & Row: New York, 1972.

Index

Genesis
17:1-8 23

Exodus
26:34 25

Numbers
13 27

Joshua
23:1-13 124
24:14-15 124

Psalms
22:3 101
95:7 126
100:4 31

Proverbs
31:10-31 120

Isaiah
2:3 34
11:1-10 74

Ezekiel
37:1-10 30

Hosea
14:1-9 118

Malachi
3:10 97

Matthew
2:1-12 81
5:3-10 37
6:6 52
6:24 95
18:20 39
20:17-18 34
22:36-40 41
28:18-20 104

Luke
2:8-20 76
2:21 78
2:22 34
2:41-52 43
3:1-14 106
5:1-11 89
8:4-15 44
10:30-37 46

Luke (*continued*)
11:5-8 49
17:11-19 100
22:17-23 109
24:1-12 83
24:13-35 112

John
1:43 53
1:43-51 52
5:17 127
6:16-21 55
14:6-7 56
15:1-11 58
20:1-18 85

1 Corinthians
8 61
11:17-34 114
12 63

Ephesians
3:14-21 107
4:1-6 21

4:11 97
6:1-3 122
6:10-17 66

Philippians
3:7 68
3:12-16 69

Colossians
3:11-17 116

1 Thessalonians
5:11 91

Hebrews
12:1 87

James
5:13-16 71

1 John
3:18 93